To Ba...
Get we...
the

BASTARDS I HAVE MET

love !
+ +

Barry Crump wrote his first book 'A Good Keen Man' in 1960. It became an immediate bestseller, as did numerous books which followed. His most famous and best-loved New Zealand character is Sam Cash, who features in, 'Hang on a Minute Mate', Crump's second book. Between them, these two books have sold over 400,000 copies and continue to sell at an amazing rate, some thirty years later.

Crump began his working life as a professional hunter, culling deer and pigs in some of the ruggedest country in New Zealand. After the runaway success of his first book, he has pursued many diverse activities, including goldmining, radio talk-back, white-baiting, television presenting, crocodile shooting, acting and numerous other activities. His face is familiar to all New Zealanders through a series of motor-vehicle commercials which have won world-wide acclaim.

He currently lives in a remote valley in the Bay of Plenty where he runs a few animals on what he describes as the smallest sheep station in New Zealand. He hopes to complete a full-feature movie in the near future and finish his latest book, another in the vivid style that has enthralled his readers for three decades. Something to look forward to for all Crump fans. As to classifying his occupation, Crump insists that, he always has been, and always will be, a Kiwi bushman.

Books by Barry Crump

A GOOD KEEN MAN (1960)*
HANG ON A MINUTE MATE (1961)*
ONE OF US (1962)
THERE AND BACK (1963)
GULF (1964)
SCRAPWAGON (1965)
THE ODD SPOT OF BOTHER (1967)
NO REFERENCE INTENDED (1968)
WARM BEER AND OTHER STORIES (1969)
A GOOD KEEN GIRL (1970)
BASTARDS I HAVE MET (1971)*
FRED (1972)
SHORTY (1980)
PUHA ROAD (1982)
THE ADVENTURES OF SAM CASH (1985)
WILD PORK AND WATERCRESS (1986)*
BARRY CRUMP BEDTIME YARNS (1988)*
BULLOCK CREEK (1989)*

* Currently in print 1990

An informal encyclopedia of some of the types of Bastard you run into these days, complete with ungarnished reports of the author's personal encounters with them, and the whole thing immeasurably enhanced by Graham Kirk's inspired drawings.

These stories are dedicated to the Bright Bastard, whoever he was, who first coined the title phrase of this priceless volume of disquisitions on Bastardry — and to those of us who know how he felt.

BASTARDS
I HAVE
MET

BARRY CRUMP

Illustrated by
Graham Kirk

'Bastards I Have Met'

Published by MOA Beckett Publishers Limited
28 Poland Road, Glenfield, Auckland, New Zealand
PO Box 100–749, North Shore Mail Centre

Copyright Barry Crump

First edition 1971
Reprints numerous
This edition 1994

Printed by McPherson's Printing Group, Australia

ISBN 0-9597897-4-X

Contents

SOME OTHER BASTARDS, IN NO PARTICULAR ORDER

He wasn't a bad poor bastard,
He'd share his only crust.
And never a better horseman
Dragged his stockwhip through the dust.

BILL

Introduction

NOW BEFORE YOU GO running away with any wild ideas about the title of this book I'd better get one thing clear — it wasn't my idea. It was suggested to me on several hundred different occasions, over the years, by several hundred different people, in several hundred different places, at several hundred different times, in several hundred different ways. A man's got to be pretty thick to ignore such a hint. So I got to thinking about it.

Then I borrowed a dictionary from the schoolmistress and looked up the word *bastard*, to see what it's supposed to mean. Here's what I found.

> **bastard, n. & a. (Child) born out of wedlock or of adultery, illegitimate; (of things) unauthorized, hybrid, counterfeit; —*file* (with serrations of medium coarseness); — *slip*, sucker of tree (also fig., = *bastard* n.); (Bot) nearly resembling another species (— BALM); (Zool.) — *wing*, rudimentary extra digit with quill-feathers. (ME,f.OF f.) *bast*. (BAT-) packsaddle (used as bed by muleteer)+ — ARD; cf. BANTLING.**

Nothing much use in that lot. One of those dictionary blokes is going to fall back into a heap of his own verbiage one of these days and smother himself.

I decided to stick to our meaning of the word, and then something occurred to me, something so glaringly obvious, so utterly simple and fundamental that it took me a quite a while to get it sorted out in my mind.

It was nothing less than a damning indictment of the very structure of our whole society. A shocking omission! No wonder the country's in an uproar! No wonder the students are playing merry hell all over the place. How can we blame the workers for striking for more pay? How inevitable that we can't understand what the devil our politicians are raving about! How inescapable that our very newspapers can't report even a simple incident or statement without getting it distorted! How right my landlady is to invade my privacy with her constant threatening demands for money! How futile to hope that they won't be forced to raise even higher the prices of such essential commodities as tobacco and beer! — When there's never been a single book or poem, or TV documentary, or song; or even a speech, devoted to the common or garden Bastard!

Do you realise that the only bastards we ever hear about are only ever there to be a kind of contrast to some scungy hero? And an exhaustive and comprehensive survey carried out by myself in the public bar of the Timberlands Hotel one Saturday afternoon reveals that bastards outnumber heroes by more than fifteen thousand to one. (This figure is very conservative and can be checked quite simply — all you have to do is go into a pub and listen).

Now, now, good reader, there's no need to mark your place and go rushing off to spread the alarm among your loved ones. The matter is under control. You see I, too, was staggered. The situation must be remedied at once!

And so, with the almost overwhelming sense of responsibility to my fellow man and posterity that the work demands of me, I hereby present, without prejudice or regard for the feelings of censors or other would-be inhibitors, this absolutely scrupulously honest, truthful, factual, unvarnished stark and courageous account of — The Bastards I Have Met.

2
Actual Bastard

IT'S ONE OF THE strange truths about Bastardry that the people we are most reluctant to call bastards are those we know to be Actual Bastards (*Bastardus fairdinkumus*). That is, people whose parents either knew themselves or each other too well to risk putting their relationship on to a more formal basis, or who didn't get to know each other well enough. After all, you just don't go round discussing marriage with comparative strangers, do you? It's not always advisable to tell them too much about your past, let alone discuss a future of wedded bliss with them.

Gordon Meltzer, a bloke I worked on the Forestry with, was an Actual Bastard, and, like most Actual Bastards, there was nothing to distinguish him from any other kind of bastard. In fact Gordon was more of an Honest Bastard (*Bastardus truthus*) than anything else. He told us once how he'd given up volunteering the information to people that he was an Actual Bastard. Not because he was ashamed of it or guilty about it, but because of *their* reactions.

The trouble with Gordon was not that his old man didn't make an honest woman out of his mother, but that he didn't stick around long enough to teach Gordon how to be *dis*honest. Gordon couldn't tell a lie to save himself. He was so honest that people often found him very disconcerting, which doesn't say much for the state of the society, or do much for getting Gordon any close mates.

I'll never forget the time our forestry boss came and told us that they'd asked him to see if any of the blokes from the planting gangs would like to apply for training as rangers. If we did we could have a day off to go in to the head office for an interview. Gordon and another bloke and I decided to have a go at it, and in we went to see Mr Blund himself, The Controller of Forests.

The office girl showed the three of us into Mr Blund's office

13

Bastardus fairdinkumus

and he sat us down and took our names. Then he asked the other bloke why he wanted to be a Forestry Ranger, and he told him, openly and frankly, how he'd always liked the open-air life; how he believed that forestry was one of the nation's most important assets and it was vital to the economy and progress of the country that it be properly administered and protected, and how he'd decided that to be a part of this great and developing industry was the most worthwhile thing he could make a career of etc. etc. etc.

You could see by the way the Controller looked at him that he was overdoing it a bit, but he waited until he'd finished. Then he said to Gordon, "And why do *you* wish to train as a ranger, Mr Meltzer?"

"I don't know, actually," said Gordon with his customary lack of deception.

"But surely you must have *some* reason for applying for it," prompted the Controller.

"Well, my mates wanted to come in and see about it," said Gordon.

"You mean you just came along to keep them company," said the Controller.

"It's a day off on full pay and a free trip into town," Gordon reminded him. It was almost as though Gordon was inviting the Controller of Forests to be in on a good thing. The C. of Fs. was looking from one to the other of us very suspiciously by this time, but there was nothing we could do to shut Gordon up. "We don't have to go back to camp until tonight," he added.

"I see," said the Controller. "So you just came in to apply for a position as a trainee ranger in order to get the day off — all of you," he added, looking at the other bloke and me. "It seems to me that you chaps have simply taken advantage of our invitation for applications to get yourselves a paid day off. Is this correct?" he said to Gordon.

"Yes," said Gordon.

That rocked the controller of Forests. He didn't get where he was by dealing in the kind of commodity Gordon was dispensing. It took him a few moments to work out how to reply to Gordon's one-word occupational suicide — or rather, suicides. There were three of us on the skids.

Maria,

3
Bad Bastard

AND NOW, LEARNED READER — fellow student of bastardry, patient peruser of these propaedeutic ponderations, Decent Bastard (*Bastardus goodblokeus*) — I cannot risk my reputation for straight-shooting, down-to-earth, commonsense and unbribable honesty. I must now deal with the category of bastard that brings to all of us the most horripulating recollections of all the worst kind of bastard we've run into.

(I'll have to return this dictionary to the schoolmistress. It's causing an element of anafractuosity to creep into this, the first and only maieutic, tendentious prolegomina yet produced on the vitally important subject of bastitudinariousness.)

But onward — you will already have gathered that the type of bastard I'm going to deal with now is the Bad Bastard (Bastardus skulduggerus).

Read this out loud: "He's a bad bastard, that one."

Louder — so you can hear it — See what I mean?

The bad bastard is a combination of every other kind of unpleasant bastard known to you and me, and between us both you've got to admit we've met a few of 'em. He even has a go at pretending to be a Decent Bastard, when he thinks it'll take genuine D.Bs. like you and me in.

Of all the abuse and condemnation, criticism and contempt, rejection and indifference that we can bring to our aid in times of exasperation and outrage, there's nothing to beat calling someone ". . . a bad bastard."

It implies that there's no hope for him. He's simply incorrigibly bad. He warrants no sympathy or attempt at rehabilitation. He's always been a bad bastard and he always will be. If he ever gets caught, and they do sometimes, or hurt, or cheated (rare), or if he simply runs into a bit of ordinary bad luck, the Bad Bastard has only got what's coming to him. He's been asking for it for

Bastardus skulduggerus

a long time. Nobody will stand by him, mainly because he doesn't bloody well deserve it.

I feel that this is an appropriate occasion to introduce you to a whole new aspect of bastardry. In these times of exaggeration, when the use of superlatives in speech is almost as common as it used to be in motion-picture advertising, we're often stumped for words when it comes to describing something that is genuinely extraordinary. Not so with bastardry. The description of any type of bastard is simply and effectively doubled by putting in front of it the word "real". A *Real* Dirty Bastard, a *Real* ugly Bastard etc. etc.

I've brought this to your notice at this point because the bloke it is my inescapable duty to tell you about now was a *Real* Bad Bastard. He was such a thorough-going bastard that if you'd seen his mother and father's marriage certificate, duly signed and dated, with his own birth certificate attached, you'd still swear it was a forgery.

I don't want you to get the idea I'm prejudiced or anything, it's just that I didn't like the look of the bastard from the moment I slapped eyes on him. It wasn't so much the way he looked, it was the way he *was*. There was something not quite right about him. He was short and stocky and grubby-looking. About thirty-five or -six, I'd say, with his hair swished straight back. When he spoke he talked without expression, as though he was reading out loud.

And there was something clammy about him. He had clammy eyes. And besides all that he whistled under his breath and rapped on the bar with the edge of a coin, half-catching your attention all the time.

He told us his name was Howard Blake, but one of the blokes told my mate Clive Piper that he'd run into him driving buses up north and he was calling himself Henry Cook there. But whatever his name was there was no doubting his B-rating. He walked into the pub one night and took three dollars off the blokes at the dart board. Then he came over and cleaned up all our best "guns" on the pool-table. And he never shouted once. Not once! He'd just get a beer and sit on it for half an hour at a time.

He turned up again the next night and got stuck into us again,

18

so some of us got our heads together and decided to have a go at getting him boozed, because it didn't look as though he could take much grog. But he drank double-whiskies and jugs of beer, on us, all night, and the only difference it made was that he started whistling as he sauntered round the pool-table sinking balls one after the other. Yes, the bastard actually *whistled*!

He got to coming in every night after that — he'd landed a job with the Ministry of Works. It wasn't long before he couldn't get us to play darts or pool with him, but there were plenty of people passing through and we used to have to watch while this cunning bastard talked them into playing pool for a jug of beer, for even as much as a dollar a game sometimes. And then he'd proceed to thrash the strides off them. Sometimes they wouldn't even get a shot, he'd sink the lot off the break, which, often as not, he'd talked them into giving him.

And on Saturdays, when he had a few under his belt, he'd start getting sarcastic. And then he'd go round acting as though he was an old mate of yours, bludging drinks and interrupting yarns and conversations.

Ted Butler told this bloke to get lost one day and he blind-hit Ted in the side of the face with a glass and cut his cheek. So Ted took the bastard outside to pin his ears back for him, once and for all, but he dropped Ted with a dirty punch in the throat while they were going out the door. And then he dropped two of the blokes who butted in to stop him putting the boot into Ted while he was on the ground. Bang! Bang! Just like that. The bloody little bastard could fight like a thrashing machine.

Then the cops arrived and we were all expecting him to get run in for assaulting Ted with the glass, but the cunning bastard talked his way out of it! That was when Stevie the barman said: "He's a Bad Bastard, that one. A Real Bad Bastard."

That was what he was all right, and he really lived up to it. He stole and bludged and cheated and got the blame and got away with it all over the district for months. He'd thieve the harness off a nightmare. We knew it was him who broke into the bottlestore of the pub one night, so did the cops, but he turned up in the pub the next night as bold as brass, trying to talk someone into a game of pool for fifty cents. And no one could do anything about it.

19

The Ministry of Works knew it was him who was selling M.O.W. diesel to the private contractors over on the hydro scheme, but when they gave him notice to quit he kicked up such a stink with the union that they had to drop the matter and keep him on. And somehow he *still* went on flogging their diesel. They never found out how he was doing it as far as I know.

And then, in the manner of all Bad Bastards, he did a moonlight. Disappeared, just like that. One night we noticed that he hadn't been into the pub for a few nights, and one of the M.O.W. blokes said that he didn't think he'd been at work either. He was gone all right, and a couple of weeks later they found out that young Judy Grimwood was four months pregnant. It was never actually proved who the father was, but we had our ideas all the same. So did old Harry Grimwood.

Goodness knows where that bloke is now, but if you ever run into a short, stocky, grubby-looking bloke, about thirty-five or -six, hair swished back and whistles under his breath and raps on the bar with the edge of a coin, half-catching your attention all the time — you want to keep out of his way, it might just be him, and he's a Real *Bad* Bastard.

4

Clever Bastard

I WAS WAITING IN the Department of Labour and Employment one day when I heard a conversation start up at a slide a bit further along from the one I was waiting at. Or I should say I heard *half* of a conversation start up, because the Labour and Employment bloke was inside the room and I couldn't hear him. But the other character's voice was as loud as his personality was. I couldn't *not* hear him.

This is how it went.

"G'day. I . . . er . . . was lookin' around for a job and they reckon you blokes are the caper so I just dropped in to see if you could put me onto something."

"— — — — — — —?" (Something from the L. and E. bloke.)

"Charlie. Charlie Roberts, but me mates usually call me Wrecker because of something that happened once."

"— — — — — — —?"

"Eighteen next month, but I can pass for twenty-two or -three easy enough."

"— — — — — — —?"

"Well I'll have a crack at just about anything. What y'got?"

"— — — — — — —?"

"Ah . . . well I haven't *been* working just lately, as a matter of fact. Been on holiday, sort of."

"— — — — — — —?"

"Let's see now . . . Must be about six weeks since I threw the last job in."

"— — — — — — —?"

"Bridge job. Over in the King Country. I was only there a couple of months. Didn't hit it off too well with the foreman."

"— — — — — — —?"

"No, nothin' like that. As a matter of fact him and me didn't see eye to eye about me trottin' his daughter round."

"— — — — — — —?"

21

Bastardus smartfartus

"Aw . . . he reckoned she was too young or something. she looked big enough to me, though. Turned out she was only fourteen or fifteen or something like that."

"— — — — — — —?"

"Cut it out! A joker can't go round asking people their age when he hardly knows 'em properly, can he?"

"— — — — — — —?"

"No, I didn't get around to asking about a reference. Never go in for 'em myself, as a matter of fact. Anyone can write himself out a reference if he wants one. I mean, if a bloke's going to give a man a reference he either gives 'im a good one or you don't bother askin' for it. No one's going to flash a crook reference around if he's after a job, now is he?"

"— — — — — — —?"

"No, they gave me a week's pay instead of notice. I was thinkin' of going to you blokes about it but I decided it wasn't worth it in the finish."

"— — — — — — —?"

"Well it wasn't only the foreman's daughter, actually. There was a bit of a stink about a truck."

"— — — — — — —?"

"Had a bit of a prang. Ran it into the ditch."

"— — — — — — —?"

"No, well as a matter of fact I wasn't actually supposed to be driving it at the time."

"— — — — — — —?"

"Funny you should mention that. I was just thinkin' of goin' in to get a licence the day after it happened. That wasn't what they really went crook about anyway."

"— — — — — — —?"

"Oh, we'd just been in to pick up a couple of bottles of booze for me mate's birthday."

"— — — — — — —?"

"No, we were dead stone cold sober."

"A couple of crates. A fair bit of it got busted and some nosey parkers came along before we could get it cleaned up properly. And you know how beer stinks when it's busted all over the place."

"— — — — — —?"

"Well it does."

"— — — — — —?"

"Well it might have been all right anyway, only one of the blokes got knocked around a bit. Probably wasn't hangin' on properly, if you ask me."

"— — — — — —?"

"Don't know exactly. Something to do with his back. They whipped him off to hospital anyway. I was a bit worried about it for a while there, as a matter of fact. I mean, I didn't know but he might have kicked the bucket of something. Them ambulance blokes won't let on what's wrong with a bloke when they take him away."

"— — — — — —?"

"Oh he's as good as gold now. Got a cushy job in the office after that, I believe. They reckon he's in for a good slice of compo. out of it. Partial disablement, they reckon. Some jokers get all the luck."

"— — — — — —?"

"Well I'm not too fussy, mate. Anything'll do me."

"— —?"

"Dairy farm? Yeah, I worked on a dairy farm for four months one time."

"— — — — — —?"

"Up north. Morrinsville."

"Funny you should mention that. The boss was a bit of a bastard, but it was his missus who wore the pants. It was her who gave me the push, as a matter of fact."

"— — — — — —?"

"Well she reckoned it was because they couldn't afford to keep me on, but I'd spotted her watchin' me teach the daughter how to ride a bike the day before she gave me the push. The old bat just didn't trust a bloke, if you ask me. It's no good workin' on a place where they don't trust a man. He's better off out of it all together . . . Where is this place, by the way?"

"— — — — — —?"

"Woodville, eh. How many cows?"

24

"— — — — — — —?"

"Sounds okay. Wouldn't mind havin' a look at it. A man can always throw it in if it's no good, can't he."

"— — — — — — —?"

"Well thanks, mate. That's mighty decent of you. What's this bloke's name?"

"— — — — — — —?"

"Boggs eh! That's a beaut."

"— — — — — — —?"

"Good. Thanks. I'll go up there tomorrow . . . They tell me you blokes'll pay a man's fare if he's stuck for cash to get to a job. That right?"

"— — — — — — —?"

"Yeah, I am as a matter of fact. Been having a crook run of luck lately."

"— — — — — — —?"

"Good, that'll do me. Thanks a lot . . . You don't happen to know if this bloke Boggs has got any daughters, do you?"

"— — — — — — —?"

"Ah well, you never know your luck."

"— — — — — — —?"

"Okay then, I'll be seein' you. Ta."

And with that, our friend slouched out of the Department of Labour and Employment, slamming the door behind him.

How's *that* for a Clever Bastard (*Bastardus smartfartus*)!

Doug

5
Dozey Bastard

YES, STAN FUDD WAS a true-blue, dyed-in-the-wool, honest-to-goodness, fair-dinkum, jumped-up-never-to-come-down, gold-plated, Dozey Bastard (*Bastardus drippus*). Not a bad truck-driver, mind you, but a Really Dozey Bastard, all the same.

I was driving trucks at the time. Big artics., long hauls. Auckland — Napier — Gisborne — Palmerston North — Wellington, runs like that, and usually two or three of us would set off together and stay more or less together as long as we could.

One day, when my mate Mike Foote and I were getting ready for a routine run down to Palmerston North and back, the boss came and introduced this new bloke, Stan Fudd, and asked us to show him the ropes and keep an eye on him. He was to drive a third rig and bring back a load of refrigerated fish.

So off we went, Mike up front, the new bloke in the middle, and I brought up the rear. It's a fairly long run down to Palmerston North but we were all empty and got there in eleven hours — one o'clock in the morning — and had a kip in our usual pub.

The new bloke could handle a truck all right, there's no doubt about that, but by the time we'd loaded up and had a feed he was looking a bit weary on it. Not used to the long runs. And by the time we'd made it back up to Taupo he was looking really beat, so we stopped for an hour to give him a spell.

Back at the depot we were told to get some sleep because there was a rush job on and we had to leave for Napier early next morning.

Stan turned up yawning and hollow-eyed and when we stopped for lunch at Taupo he almost went to sleep at the cafe table we were sitting at. So Mike went to his truck and came back with a jar of tablets he kept in his cab.

"Here, take one of these," he said to Stan. "It'll keep you awake."

26

Bastardus drippus

"What are they?" said Stan.

"Methedrines," said Mike. "They'll stop you going to sleep on the road. There's a rough stretch between here and Napier and we don't want you going over the bank."

"Okay, thanks," said Stan, taking one of the pills and washing it down with coffee.

"You'd better take a few of these," said Mike, pouring about fifty of them onto a table napkin for him. "Just take one when you feel yourself getting sleepy."

"Thanks," said Stan. "I need something like that."

"You have to be careful not to take too many of them," warned Mike.

But I don't think Stan can have heard him — or perhaps it was just that he was a Dozey Bastard — because he took to those methedrine pills like nobody's business. He drove non-stop to Napier and didn't even wait until morning to head back.

I was trying to sleep in the same hotel room as him and he flounced and creaked around in his bed for a couple of hours and then he got dressed and went out for a walk around. He woke me up in the early hours of the next morning to tell me he was going to head on back to Auckland.

His truck was in the yard, unloaded, serviced and ready to take off again, by the time Mike and I arrived back late that night. And when we met at the depot two days later, Stan, hollow-eyed and wildly excited, whispered hoarsely to us (although there was nobody else within earshot) that he hadn't been to sleep since he'd got back from Napier but he felt terrific.

"I've been having long discussions with the wife," he confided to us. "Our whole lives have been changed!"

"You want to take it a bit easy on those methedrines," Mike told him. "You'll go right off if you keep taking too many of them."

"I've hardly touched them!" protested Stan quickly, looking guiltily around the yard.

"Just take it easy, all the same," said Mike. "Give them a rest for a few days."

Stan got held up at the depot that morning so Mike and I left ahead of him, but he passed us later in the day, grim-jawed and

28

black-eyed, heading south as though he was in an army tank or a jumbo-jet.

He got out of step with us, we couldnt keep up with him. He was making half as much again as us, and we were on big money.

Then the jar of methedrines disappeared out of Mike's truck and we started getting worried. We asked Stan about it and he accused us of picking on him — just like his wife had been lately.

"He won't be able to keep it up," Mike said to me. "It won't be long before it catches up on him."

And it wasn't. We'd caught up with Stan at an eating place well down the line and were having one of our rare meals together. But Stan wasn't hungry and picked at the edges of his food as though he'd already eaten too much, but he drank five cups of coffee and then drank all the milk out of the jug on our table. We tried to talk to him but he was almost incoherent by this time. Raving wildly for a few minutes and then lapsing suddenly into a sullen brooding silence. And before Mike and I had finished eating he abruptly left us, saying as he went that he had to get going.

We decided that if he got any worse we'd have to get the boss to lay him off for a few days. It didn't look to us as though Stan had been eating or sleeping anywhere near enough over the past couple of weeks (ever since the methedrines) and we estimated that he'd lost between a stone and a half and two stone in weight.

It was about half past one the following morning when we came up to Stan's truck, stopped in the middle of the road on a long straight, with the motor running and the lights on full-beam and the cab door hanging open. There were fifty-yard-long black streaks of rubber on the road where he'd slammed on his brakes at high speed. It's a wonder he hadn't jack-knifed her.

We pulled over and stopped our trucks and got out to look for Stan. We'd gone past him. He was back up the road looking around in some fern down the bank, lighting matches and calling out, "Hoi, Hoi there! Where are you?"

It was just as well it was us who'd found him. We led him back to the trucks and made him drink some coffee from the thermos I carried in my cab.

And this, as near as we could gather, was what had happened

29

to him. He was just driving along making good time when the little naked man who'd been scampering along in his headlights with his umbrella up for about forty or fifty miles suddenly disappeared with a scream under the front of the truck. Stan stamped on his brakes and jammed the 22-ton rig to a hell of a stop but there was no hope for the little man. By the time we'd arrived Stan had searched through the tyres and wheels of his outfit and right back up the road, but there was no sign of him.

We found twenty-six of the two hundred-odd methedrines he'd nicked from Mike's truck in his shirt pocket and had no conscience about confiscating them. Then we shifted Stan's truck to a safe place off the road and locked it up and took him about 40 miles to our nearest stopping hotel and put him to bed.

He slept for a day and a night and was looking a little better when we picked him up on our way back and drove him to pick up his truck. He was a day and a half late getting back to the depot but we'd organised a breakdown yarn for him and he didn't get into trouble over it.

"Not that he didn't deserve to," said Mike. "Us long-distance drivers have been using methedrines for ten years that I know of, and they're a damn good thing if you use them sensibly. But it only takes someone like Stan to get everyone calling them dangerous drugs. Anything'd be dangerous in the hands of a Dozey Bastard like that."

And you have to admit that Mike was right. A Dozey Bastard.

6

Enigmatic Bastard

I DON'T THINK IT'D be too presumptuous of me to describe Suggy Benson as an Enigmatic Bastard (*Bastardus perplexus*). The only Real Enigmatic Bastard I've ever run into, as a matter of fact. There's been so much talk flying around about him that it's got right out of hand altogether, so I've decided to set the facts down while there's still time, and then people will be able to form their own opinions about him.

Though I personally knew Suggy as well as just about anybody (he's dead just now) I still can't make up my mind about him. There's those who say he was nothing but a lazy, shiftless, selfish criminal, with no regard for anybody else — or their property. And then there's those who swear that Suggy was a thoughtful, considerate friend to anyone in trouble; a Good Bastard. Only rob people who could afford it. A 'Robin Hood' kind of bloke.

I don't know — both sides of the story are true enough, I suppose. All I know is that if you were with Suggy Benson you were all right. You'd never go short of a feed or somewhere to sleep, or even a job, if you wanted one. He had bunks all over the country, did Suggy. There was the university gymnasium and the hothouse and one or two other places in Auckland. The Te Rapa racetrack buildings in Hamilton. Hot pools at Rotorua and Taupo. A church and a school in Wellington. Railway carriages and one or two other little spots in Christchurch. And a lean-to that backed right up against a baker's ovens in Dunedin. Just to mention a few of the more obvious ones.

And wherever he went he had his own special lurk for getting a feed. Never knew him to go hungry, old Suggy, and he went through a few rough spots, believe me. For absolute emergencies, for example, there were the Albert Park goldfish in Auckland. Trout in Rotorua and Taupo. Pigeons in Wellington and Dunedin. And ducks in Rotorua and Christchurch — to mention a careful few. Yes, Suggy could swipe a duck or pigeon or goldfish —

31

Bastardus perplexus

anything you liked — from right under your nose and you'd never know it was happening.

You see, Suggy Benson was the most terrific thief you ever saw in all your born days. If he wanted something it'd never occur to him to go and buy it, or ask for it, or anything like that. He'd just swipe it. And he'd swipe it so naturally that quite often eyewitnesses wouldn't realise what he was doing.

The thing about Suggy's pinching was that he didn't seem to mind whether he got caught or not. They reckon no one will ever know exactly how much stuff Suggy knocked-off in his time. He seemed to have a genius for lifting the kind of stuff you don't miss for a while, and then you wonder just when it went off, and whether someone might have borrowed it — or what the hell had happened to it.

It wasn't always like that though. For instance there was the time Suggy pinched a whole truckload of Maoris. They were on their way from Ruatahuna to Ngaruawahia for a *tangi*, with one of their cousins in a coffin under some sacks on the back of the truck. They pulled up at the Murupara pub and the driver and his mate went in to leave a message with one of their other cousins and they got held up in there. Suggy wandered out of the pub a bit later and noticed the truck parked there with all the flax baskets and blankets and old ladies and kids on board. So he hopped in and drove the whole caboodle back to Ruatahuna. Everyone on the truck thought they were going back to pick up some people, or something that had been left behind.

When they got there Suggy pulled up outside the store and wandered off without saying anything to anyone, and it was hours before they livened that something might be up. And when it was all sorted out nobody knew what to do about it. They reported it to the local cop when they got back from the *tangi* about a week later, but he didn't believe them so they let it slide. No one thought to mention it to Suggy. It wouldn't have seemed to be worth making an issue of, I suppose, especially once they got talking to him.

And while they were away at the *tangi* Suggy had moved in with one of the families and was almost a relative by the time they got back. But don't run away with the idea that those Maoris were suckers, or dumb, or anything like that. The Passenger Transport Company found themselves in exactly the same kind of position the time Suggy drove one of their buses out of the city terminal and spent the whole afternoon picking up people around the suburbs and running them into town, or wherever else they wanted to go. Then he put the bus back where he'd got it from and it was a week before they found out it had been taken.

The first the company heard about it was when they got a letter from Suburban Buses Ltd. asking them to explain what an Otahuhu Bus had been doing on their North Shore run a couple of days before. They hadn't even missed the bus and eventually decided that the best thing they could do was tighten up on their security a bit and hush the matter up as best they could, to try and save themselves the embarrassment of an enquiry into how someone could have used one of their buses for a whole afternoon and then put it back without being spotted.

One of the things about Suggy was that he looked so *innocent*, even when he was actually in the act of whipping something. There was the time he scored three bolts of high-class suit material from a department store: Suggy had been in there getting a new pair of socks for himself and he was just leaving when a bloke staggered in the door with a big parcel. Suggy thought it might be blankets and it was getting on for winter, so he pulled the bloke up. "I'll take that," he said to him. "Okay," said the bloke. "Sign here." So Suggy signed something and took the bolts of cloth. When he found out what it was he gave someone one of the bolts in return for making the other two bolts up into blankets for him.

They put Suggy on probation once, but he never bothered reporting. The probation officer picked him up from the billiard room one afternoon and drove him round to the probation office and spent about half an hour tearing strips off him. Suggy promised to be a good boy in future, walked out of there, hopped into the probation officer's car on Friday night and put it back on Sunday afternoon, when he got back to town. And he never heard another word about it.

It seems that when the probation officer came out and found the car gone he didn't do anything about it because two of the other probation officers had the use of the same car. When the three of them got together later in the week to try and work out which one of them had clocked up six hundred and forty-one miles over the weekend, of course they all denied *having* the car on the weekend. And each of them was convinced that one of the others was lying, the real truth never occurred to them. The nature of their work had evidently made them distrustful of everyone, including each other.

And so it went. Suggy spent his whole life being casually disinterested in anything to do with the due order and course of anything he happened to come into contact with. He was quite indifferent to the precedents and standards of the system; absolutely unaffected by prescriptions, or formulas, examples, customs, methods, routines, norms, tenets, commandments, conventions, codes, recipes, regimes, precepts or discretions.

Of course a man who ignores everything consistent with order and routine isn't going to have an easy time of it. Suggy certainly didn't. I happen to know that the one year the Income Tax people collared him they discovered to their horror that he could only remember twenty-six of the jobs he'd had during the preceding financial year.

"But that's an average of less than two weeks on each job!" the Income Tax Bloke said to him.

"I've got an idea I put in a few days driving for a firewood bloke in the King Country," recalled Suggy helpfully. "Can't remember what his name was, though. In fact I'm not quite sure whether it was last year or the year before. . . ."

Suggy fought in the Second World War, you know. Too right! And I heard that from the time he was called up until his outfit arrived in the Middle East every bit of Suggy's leave was cancelled because of his continuous casual attitude towards army regulations. Every bit of his *official* leave, that is. Some of his mates used to swear that he was A.W.O.L. for more of the time than he was there for his C.O. to confine to barracks. They only just got him onto the boat in time to ship him overseas (they'd finally found him shoeing a horse before he left for a mate of his who had a crook back).

Once they'd actually got Suggy over there and out into the desert where all the action was, his record changed dramatically, and yet his behaviour remained exactly the same as it always was. He was wounded twice and returned himself to front-line duty twice. He was captured once, and immediately escaped, and returned himself to the front lines again.

He was mentioned in despatches a number of times mainly for his level-headedness and calm courage under heavy enemy attack. One officer reported that, against direct orders, Private Benson deliberately left his post and advanced across eighty yards of open terrain under heavy enemy fire, disabled an enemy tank by climbing up and dropping a hand-grenade through the hatch, and then returned, unhurt, to his post. This action undoubtedly enabled them to hold their position, but the officer requested advice on how to deal with Private Benson for disobeying a direct order from his superior officer.

One of Suggy's mates said to me, years later, "He was a brave bastard all right. A Real Brave Bastard (*Bastardus heroicus*), there's no doubt about that. It's a wonder he didn't get himself killed half a dozen times over."

In fact Suggy was recommended for the V.C. three times, but each time they tried to present him with the thing they found out that he was due to come up for court martial for something or other, and by the end of the war the two things had eventually cancelled themselves out. His discharge was honourable, as it bloody well should have been.

A lot of people might have said that Suggy shouldn't have done a lot of those things; that he was breaking the law and ought to have been punished for it; that he was a bit of a Bad Bastard. But before you make up your mind one way or the other, I think you should know a bit about Suggy's background. You see, I went to school with Suggy for a while, and I don't know anything about psychology but I think what I have to tell you might throw some light on why he was like he was and did the things he did.

As far as we could find out, Suggy had been left behind at his Uncle Charlie's place at the end of the Christmas holidays, and he was staying on there because they had trouble keeping a farmhand on the place. We were both ten or eleven years old at the time, in the same class at school, Suggy was waiting at the end of Boundary Road with the Wallace kids on the day school started for the year and he came in on the school bus and told Mr Fusk his parents wanted him to get to our school for that year because of family arrangements. That's all you had to do to get into a school in those days. Getting out of them was a different matter.

They were only about thirty-five kids at the school and everyone, from standard one up to standard six, was taught in the same room by the headmaster, Mr Fusk, and nobody liked him. In fact he was a Real Rotten Bastard (*Bastardus putrefactus*). He quickly nosed out the kids who could be persecuted without the risk of them getting too much sympathy at home, and he had Suggy sorted out within a couple of days of him starting at the school. On the third day he called him out in front of the whole school and went through his hair with two pencils held like a knife and fork. Then he dropped the pencils into the waste paper basket with an exaggerated air of disgust and told him to go and sit down again.

And he soon found out that Suggy was liable to get into trouble if he was late home from school, so he always kept him in to punish him for real or imagined breaches of his regulations. The school bus was too small to take all the kids from out our way in one load and had to make two trips of it. If Suggy was held back till the second trip he could usually just make it home in time for the milking by running like hell through Wallace's place. I don't think Fusk ever found out about that. By this time we were all on Suggy's side. He didn't say much when Fusk started in on him and most of us older blokes reckoned that Fusk was going to have the new bloke broken before he was finished.

Now I'm going to have to tell you about one of the girls in standard two — you'll see why later on. This girl was so nervous of Fusk that she would usually wet herself if he kept at her long enough. When this happened he'd make her stand up on her desk while he strutted back and forth apologising to the rest of us for having to ask us to study in the company of "this — this disgusting thing."

Yes, Fusk was a Rotten Bastard all right, and that's what started Suggy talking to him. It was just after lunchtime one Friday and Fusk had had that girl I've been telling you about standing on

37

her desk for about twenty minutes and he was going to get stuck into her any minute. We all knew it. And then Suggy put up his hand and kept it up until Fusk said: "Well, Benson. What is it?"

"Please sir, some of the boys aren't paying attention sir."

"Er . . . yes, Benson. Any boys who can't answer questions at the end of the period will be kept in. Now sit down, thank you Benson."

But Suggy evidently wasn't ready to sit down yet.

"It's hard to concentrate when some of the boys aren't paying attention sir," he said.

"Yes, I'm sure it is, Benson. Now sit down and we'll get on with it."

I just wanted you to know, sir, that I like Social Studies very much, sir. And when some of the boys aren't . . ."

"Yes, Benson. Now sit *down* please!"

"I hope I haven't made you angry or anything, sir. I was just trying to help, sir."

"Yes, Benson. Now that's enough, I don't want to hear another word about it. Sit down!"

"I didn't mean to make you wild, sir. I was only . . ."

"Benson! Sit down this instant!"

"Yes, sir," said Suggy still standing, "I'm very sorry, sir. I didn't mean to make you angry with me, sir. Because I think you're the best teacher I've ever had, sir, and when some of the boys . . ."

"Leave the room, Benson! Get out of it! Go on, leave this room at once! Get out!" He was fair livid by this time.

"Yes sir," said Suggy. "Shall I take my book, sir?"

"What book?"

"My social studies exercise book, sir. This one."

"Yes, yes! Take the thing and get out!"

"Yes sir," said Suggy. And at the door of the room he stopped and said, "Sir?"

"What!" shouted Fusk.

"Where shall I go, sir?"

"Anywhere! Just get out of my sight! Go on! Out!"

"I just thought there might be something you'd like me to do outside for you, sir."

"Just get out! Get out! Get out!" shouted Fusk, slapping at his table with a book. "Get out and stay out!"

Suggy went out and then popped his head back round the door and said, "When shall I come back, sir?"

The "boys who weren't paying attention" thoroughly enjoyed Suggy's interruption, or perhaps I should say *dis*ruption, of Fusk's dreary social studies class. And Fusk had more on his mind than dealing with us, even if he could find out who we were or if we really hadn't been paying attention. And the girl he was getting ready to embarrass everyone with was spared from him that time. In fact she got to be spared quite a lot by Suggy's interventions, as time went on. Fusk would start on the girl, and Suggy would immediately say something like, "Sir?"

"Now, Benson. I'm warning you, boy. I'm in no mood for any of your impertinence . . ."

"No sir," interrupted Suggy. "It's just that I've found your notebook."

"Where?"

"Up there, sir," said Suggy, pointing to the corner of Fusk's missing notebook, just visible under a pile of maps on top of the cupboards.

"How did it get there, Benson?"

"I don't know, sir. I just noticed it. Just now, sir."

And Fusk would say, "By heaven, Benson, if I thought for a moment . . ."

And once again Fusk's attention would have been diverted from little Janice Weedborne. And Fusk hated Suggy more than ever. We all knew that if Fusk ever got one over on Suggy it'd be too bad for Suggy, but he went on baiting Fusk, even when he didn't need to. I remember once when we were out in the playground and Fusk came stalking around to put a stop to any fun that might be going on. He came near the game we were playing and Suggy went up to him and said, "Sir?"

"What is it this time, Benson?" said Fusk with the nervous twitch of his right wrist he'd developed since he'd met Suggy.

"Are you very well-to-do sir?"

39

"Don't be impertinent, boy. I've warned you about that sort of thing."

"My Aunt Meredith told me that well-to-do people always know things, sir, and I thought you must be very well-to-do because of you knowing such a lot of things, sir."

"I'm not interested in what your Aunt Meredith says, Benson. And I'll thank you not to speak to me about personal matters in the future. Now go and pick up that piece of paper and put it in the rubbish basket."

"I think it might be Brian Laing's, sir" said Suggy.

"I didn't ask you whose it was, Benson. Just put it in the rubbish basket! And don't bother me again!"

"Don't you like talking to me, sir?"

"I'll talk to you if you don't do as you're told at once, Benson. Now jump to it!'"

"I'm very sorry, sir," said Suggy. "I was only . . ."

"You think you're clever, don't you Benson. I warn you, boy, if I ever have any more of this impertinence from you I'm going to report you to the school inspectors — and your Aunt."

And Fusk turned and walked stiffly away towards the school building. At the steps he turned unexpectedly and caught us all grinning. It wasn't going to be a very pleasant afternoon for any of us, but it was well worth it. Suggy was our school hero by this time and whatever he did was okay as far as we were concerned.

Within fifteen minutes of us sitting down for the afternoon lessons Fusk had Janice Weedborne standing on her desk for being too slow getting her books out. He left her there for a while and then walked over and looked her up and down as though she was bouncing. There was a hush and then he suddenly barked, "What are you standing up there for, you idiot?"

Janic Weedborne began to climb down from the desk. Then Fusk said, "Don't you answer your teacher when he asks you a question?"

"Yes sir," she said.

"Well answer me then," he shouted. "What are you standing up there for?"

"Because you told me to, sir,"

"And did I tell you to get down again?"

"No, sir," she whispered.

"Well you'd better get down before you make another of your disgusting messes. I can't ask respectable people to sit among that kind of filth, now can I?" he demanded

Then Suggy spoke up from the back of the room.

"Please, sir. I think your dog's been sick under Troughton's desk, sir."

Fusk turned slowly. "Has he now, Benson. Well you can have the pleasure of cleaning it up."

"Yes, sir," said Suggy. "Isn't your dog very well, sir?"

"What are you talking about?" said Fusk sarcastically.

"Well it's got stuff coming out one of its ears, sir. And . . ."

"You will stay in after school this afternoon, Benson, and write on the blackboard two hundred times 'I will not speak in class unless I am spoken to,' you understand?"

And so it went, until the incident of the school bus. Somebody threw an apple-core at somebody else and it just missed the bus driver and caused him to swerve across the road. Somebody yelled out that Suggy Benson threw it and he was put off the bus to walk home. Next morning at school Fusk was a strutting figure of pompous concern. He assembled the whole school, all thirty-eight of us, in the main room and then stalked thoughtfully back and forth across the front of the room looking grim.

"It has been reported to me," he boomed, "that one of our pupils here has, by an act of complete irresponsibility, seriously endangered the lives of a number of you. Not to mention our bus driver, whose presence of mind we have to thank for the fact that some of us," (he lowered his voice) "are here today."

A long pause, then, "Benson, stand out here."

Suggy went up the front and Fusk said to him, "Benson, since you have so grossly abused the facilities provided for you, I have no option but to deny them to you. You will no longer use the school transport."

"But sir, I never threw that apple," said Suggy.

"Don't you think you've done enough already, Benson, without calling your teacher and your schoolmates liars!" said Fusk quietly.

41

"But sir. . . !"

"That will do, Benson,"

Fusk turned sadly back to the rest of us standing in the hall. "And if there is any further trouble of this kind from Benson I will be forced to expel him from this school. I would ask you all to report to me at once if anything of this nature occurs again. Your lives are too important for me to ignore the risk involved in permitting this — this wretched fellow to remain in our midst unless he changes his dangerous ways. That will be all, thank you, Benson."

At the back of the hall Colin Martin started crying in his hands. And the next day Colin Martin's father came to the school and talked to Fusk out in the corridor. Then Fusk brought him into the classroom looking flustered. We knew what it was all about; quite a few of the kids knew it was Colin Martin who had thrown that apple core in the bus, and we'd had a "talk" to him about it the day before.

"It seems," began Fusk, "that young Colin has admitted to Mr Martin here that he was responsible for throwing the apple core that — er — narrowly missed the bus driver on Tuesday afternoon. It was — er — very — er — courageous of the lad to come forward like this. And it was very kind of Mr Martin to spare his valuable time to come along and — er — help us clear the matter up. In the meantime I will have to decide what is to be done about it. Apparently the lad was trying to throw the apple core out the window and it — er — it bounced . . ."

I was there that afternoon when Suggy came up to Fusk in the playground.

"What do you want, Benson?" said Fusk.

"I just wondered if it was all right for me to use the school bus again, sir."

"You will use the school bus when I say you can," snarled Fusk. "And don't think I've forgotten this. Now get out of it!"

So Suggy went on walking three and a half miles to and from school every day. By cutting across the paddocks he wasn't far behind the school bus and I don't think his aunt and uncle ever found out he'd been kicked off the bus, but somehow all the sting seemed to have gone out of him. Some of us were a bit worried in case Fusk had broken his spirit. He even seemed to have given up Fusk-baiting. Then one morning the school inspector arrived on a routine visit. I still remember him — a bony, bustling little man with a sharp nose, voice and Adam's-apple. He put his suitcase on Fusk's desk and said.

"Morning, children. Everything all right? You can sit down."

We all sat down, except Suggy. He just stayed standing up and we knew that this was going to be *it* as far as Suggy and Fusk went.

"No, sir. Everything's not all right, sir," said Suggy in a clear voice.

The inspector stopped looking through the roll and looked at Suggy for a few moments.

"I beg your pardon?" he said to him.

"I have a complaint, sir."

The inspector turned to Fusk. "Who is this boy, Mister Fusk?'"

"Benson, sir," said Fusk frowning. "One of our most difficult boys, I'm afraid. He unfortunately . . ."

"Yes, yes," said the inspector. "You say you have a complaint, Benson."

"Yes, sir."

"Well, what is this complaint?"

"There's a dog in the classroom, sir. It smells something awful and I think it's unhealthy."

"A dog, you say?" And we could see right away that this particular inspector didn't like them.

"Yes, sir."

"Where is the animal?"

"It's over here, sir," said a boy in the far corner.

And Fusk's dog was shoved out from under the desk and shooed up the aisle. An old, old, spaniel, with patches of bare hide where the hair had fallen out of him, and weeping blind eyes and cankery deaf ears. The inspector was openly horrified.

"Who let this in here? Who does it belong to, Mister Fusk?"

"He's mine," said Fusk uncomfortably.

"Take it at once from this room," ordered the inspector. "And don't let it within the school grounds again. I advise you to have the — it put away."

The inspector turned away from the sight of Fusk picking up

43

his stinking dog and carrying it awkwardly out the door. Suggy was still standing at his desk.

"Thank you, Benson. You were quite right in reporting that to me. I'll see that you aren't criticised for it. You may sit down."

"There's another matter, sir," said Suggy.

There has never been a quieter schoolroom than ours was for the few moments after Suggy said that. Then the inspector began to get a bit annoyed with him.

"Well, what is it this time?" he said impatiently.

"I've been unjustly treated at this school," said Suggy.

The inspector tapped on the desk thoughtfully for a while.

I see," he said, looking around. "Do any of you others consider that you've been unjustly treated?"

No one spoke up. The inspector looked back at Suggy.

"I hope you realise that you are liable to be severely punished for falsely claiming that your schoolteacher has mistreated you, Benson. It's a very serious charge to make."

"Yes, sir. I know," said Suggy.

He was magnificent, none of us had ever heard anyone speak to a *school inspector* like this. And none of us ever heard it again, either.

Then Fusk walked back into the room and saw Suggy still standing and the inspector looking cold and grim.

"Mister Fusk. This boy claims he has been unjustly treated here. I think we should dismiss the rest of the pupils while I hear what he has to say."

So Fusk sent everyone except Suggy into the playground with instructions to play quietly. Then he waited in the corridor while Suggy told the inspector all about it. Suggy must have been making a good fist of it too, because it took a long time. Then they sent out for Colin Martin. He came back and sent Janice Weedborne in. Then two or three others, mostly prefects and things. Then Suggy himself came out and told a livid Fusk that the inspector wanted to see him, sir.

We played around till after lunchtime and then Fusk came out and told us the whole school was dismissed for the day. We could go home. Suggy rode in the school bus and nobody would have anything to do with him, just in case.

44

And next morning Fusk was gone. There was a relieving lady teacher called Miss Gurney, who turned to be as soft as Fusk had been hard. We gave her hell, looking back on it. Reaction for Fusk, I suppose.

But the funny thing about it all was that Suggy could have been a hero and he wouldn't be, no matter how hard we pressed him. He could have been the leader of any gang he wanted. He could have been best-friends with anyone around, but he wouldn't. He wasn't even particularly interested in Janice Weedborne, who we knew was the cause of Suggy starting on Fusk in the first place.

The reason I've told you all this is because it strikes me as worth pointing out that the same can be said of most of us. You see, whether he could have changed his attitude towards things or not, Suggy never did. He responded to the army exactly as he responded to Fusk when he was a young bloke at school, and the same as everything else he ever did. He was a hero on some occasions, and, for doing exactly the same things, a villain on others. And sometimes he was a villain at the time and a hero later, and vice versa.

I suppose you could say that he was everything, good *and* bad, that everyone who knew him claims he was. At different times, of course, just like the rest of us.

If you ask me that's a pretty good reason why we ought to try and give up judging each other on one performance, usually the kind of performance that it suits us to believe of the person under judgement. It doesn't make sense when you think about it. And yet we all do it, every one of us, all the time — even such hand-picked and faultless bastards as you and I.

In fact the only person I ever knew who didn't pass judgements on people was a bloke called Suggy Benson.

Johon

7

Filthy Bastard

MOST OF US KNOW the difference between the Dirty Bastard and your actual Filthy Bastard only too well. But for the benefit and enlightenment of those who don't know I'll touch briefly on the subject.

Your Dirty Bastard (*Bastardus begrimus*) is simply unfastidious. He's often malodorous, fusty, mucky, scummy or dreggy. He may even be a little mangy, but your actual Filthy Bastard (*Bastardus filthus*) leaves him for dead. A Filthy B. is downright unwholesome. He's offensive and insanitary, feculent, scorbutic, pestilential, verminous, impetiginous, leprous, louse-bound, fly-blown and gangrenous. He's often inclined to be a little sickly as well.

And such a man was old Yorky Spudding. A Filthy B. of the first order. His existence was justified if only because he could be used as an example of how filthy a man can get if he devotes himself wholeheartedly to it for long enough.

Yorky was a pig-farmer and it's a fairly safe bet that few other occupations could have enhanced his aura as well as this one did. And apart from telling you that the cleanest things around there were the pigs, I won't describe Yorky's piggery or the way he maintained it. Such things don't only defy accurate description, but there's no point in upsetting everyone.

Yorky himself had the usual attributes of the fully-qualified Filthy Bastard. He was as filthy as he looked, or looked as filthy as he was, whichever way you cared to look at him. Creased, wrinkled, ragged, caked, clogged, cluttered, smeared, splashed and maggot-gagging. You could tell from a hundred and fifty yards away that he was a genuine gold-plated Filthy Bastard, and if you were down-wind you'd be cheating. If he hadn't been so obviously authentic you'd have sworn they'd spared no effort or expense to have him made-up for a horror movie.

And this brings me to the odour of him. Though odour is not

Bastardus filthus

the word for it. In fact an exhaustive search of the schoolmistress's dictionary brings to light no adequate language to describe the way old Yorky stank. Words like nauseous or fetid fall far short of doing justice to the almost audible fermentation of the way Yorky and his environment ponged.

There was a rumour, probably true, that Yorky's ten acres had once been in the Borough and they'd fought for years until they got the boundary shifted so he'd be in the Country.

One of the things about Filthy Bastards is that they themselves never seem to think there's anything wrong with the way they are. And Yorky was no exception to this. Take the way he never gave up advertising for a housekeeper, for example. He put literally hundreds of ads in the newspapers for a "Housekeeper to care for middle-aged farmer and light farm duties. Live in, etc. . . . . Very few of the housekeepers who came to be interviewed for the position ever got out of the taxi at Yorky's gate, and none of them ever spent the night there.

I know I haven't mentioned anything about what Yorky actually *did* to get himself into such an outrageous condition and keep himself in it, but common decency prevents me from describing the Filthy Bastard in greater detail than I have done already. You wouldn't thank me, gentle reader — Hygienic Bastard (*Bastardus sterilizus*) — for going into greater detail about old Yorky. I did note down details of a number of his more well-known escapades and activities, but it was no good. No matter how I tried to temper the acrid material I had to work with, I eventually had to discard it altogether, for fear I'd be accused of exaggerating his filthiness in order to shock my readers.

I make no apologies for moving hastily on to more wholesome subjects.

Darryl

8

Good Bastard

YOU HAVE TO BE very careful calling someone a Good Bastard. (*Bastardus virtuus*). We can all be Good Bastards when we feel like it and a convenient occasion presents itelf, but to be a Good Bastard all the time, whatever the circumstances, isn't so easy. In fact Real Good Bastards are pretty rare.

The only bastard I ever met who I could honestly say was a *good* one was Mr Jeffries. He lived in the district I was brought up in, and that's about as close as he and I ever got.

He was always polite and considerate and as far as I know he was never known to utter a derogatory remark about anyone in his whole bloody life. He went to church religiously, worked hard, kept a nice garden and always had a gift and a cheery word for anyone who was sick or hard-up or down on their luck. He mowed lawns for old ladies — and kept it up for years. He passed the hat round whenever there was a reason or a chance to. He could be relied upon absolutely and was very active in charity drives and appeals.

He was a great driving-force behind the local Civil Defence Organisation, but there's no doubt that if there *had* been an emergency involving the Civil Defence (and there never was) Mr J. would have been kept well out of it. He was far too good to have been any use in a real emergency.

He was a member of every committee, guild, fraternity, move-ment, circle, fellowship, brigade, group and panel that couldn't find an excuse to exclude him. And he got more mail than any other private individual I ever knew. He must have written thousands of letters to people all over the world, all of them good ones, of course. In fact Mr J. was so downright bloody good that no one could stand him. Even such spare-time Good Bastards as professional ecclesiastics and dedicated social workers would unashamedly groan aloud their exasperation, in the hearing of anyone who happened to be within earshot, whenever they saw

Bastardus virtuus

that an encounter with the good Mr Jeffries could not be avoided.

Children found him dull and boring and were often quite rude to him, but, being a Real Good Bastard, Mr J. never complained or retaliated or gave up being nice to them. His few and lukewarm friends treated him abominably, but he made excuses for them. His boss promoted men from under and around him, and Mr Jeffries always congratulated them warmly.

In the finish his wife couldn't stand it any longer and she up and left him without even bothering to tell him why, and, like a true Good Bastard, Mr J. took the blame.

Even the Jehovah's Witnesses found that there was nothing they could teach him about human goodness. The only kind of person I could think of who would be able to take the good Mr J.'s goodness would have to be someone as good as himself, and although I've kept a wary eye out for them all my life I've never come across another one. But then it's not likely that I'm moving in the right circles for that kind of thing these days.

It'd be nice to be able to tell you that Mr Jeffries eventually reaped the rewards of his long lifetime of service to his fellow man, but, alas, I have to report that he was carried off during an epidemic by a squadron of Asian-flu germs, against whom he'd never so much as uncorked a bottle of vapour-rub or fired a salvo of aerosol in his whole virtuous life.

I wonder where he is now. I somehow can't see him or heaven gaining anything by his residence there, but then the other place doesn't seem right for him either. Perhaps there's a special kind of halfway-house where Good Bastards go when they pass on, where they can spend their days being as good to each other as they like without anyone getting embarrassed about it. I hope so.

George

9

Hard-case Bastard

WHICH BRINGS US TO the Hard-case Bastard (*Bastardus waggus*). Everyone knows him. He's widely distributed throughout the various strata of society, though he usually prefers the working-class environment. He's often found in the drinking-schools, parties, working gangs, and generally wherever people gather together. In fact it's a measly group indeed that hasn't got its Hard-case to liven things up a bit.

His size ranges from small and weedy to big, fat and benign, and he's often referred to as "the life and soul of the party".

One of the characteristics of the H-c. B. is his inability to endure inactivity or silence, and from the time he wakes up in the morning until he finally crashes at night (often from sheer exhaustion) he's continually on the go. Playing tricks, taking the micky out of the boss, teasing people, and generally organising unusual and often hilarious departures from the normal course of things.

One of the most remarkable attributes of the Hard-case Bastard is his memory for jokes, and when he's not actually actively engaged in some other kind of hard-casery he keeps up an almost continuous running patter of jokes from his seemingly inexhaustible fund of them.

In fact one soon learns not to try telling a joke when there's a H-c. Bastard around because he won't even wait for the laughter from your joke to die down properly before he launches into one of his own. Usually the same type of joke as yours (e.g. Dad and Dave; Englishman, Irishman and Scotsman; Bill Smith and the Pope etc. etc.) whatever it is, but it's always a so much *better* joke than yours. So much better-told and up-to-date, and so much funnier than your pathetic effort, that you feel ashamed of yourself for having had the appalling bad form to try and put one across in the first place.

Fortunately it doesn't usually matter as much as it might do, because once started on a joke-telling session, the Hard-case

Bastardus waggus

Bastard can only be stopped by one of two things: (a) the breaking-up of the group, or (b) the intrusion of something on the group's attention with at least the impact of a power-cut (e.g. the beer running out). As for a genuine Hard-case Bastard running out of jokes — it doesn't happen.

One of the Hard-case Bastards I knocked around with for a while was undoubtedly the very best joke-teller I ever knew — Willy Driver. If we were in a restaurant Willy'd come up with one about a restaurant. If we saw a dog he'd come up with the one about why a dog cocks his leg — or one of the dozens he seemed to have at his very tongue-tip.

He had jokes for every occasion and I never saw him stumped for one, or even hesitate. Doctor jokes, lawyer jokes, travelling salesman jokes, tramp jokes, gangster jokes, mad-house jokes, man-falling-from-a-skyscraper jokes, Indian chief jokes, hospital jokes, chemist-shop jokes, Young Johnny jokes, Eskimo jokes, eunuch jokes, psychologist jokes, prostitute jokes, corny jokes, sick jokes, clean and hairy-dog jokes. And I must say I don't remember him ever telling the same joke twice.

Typical of Hard-case Bastards, Willy was rarely in *serious* trouble with the authorities, but on the other hand he was rarely far off it. He seemed to be always on his last chance with someone or other, or being warned that if it happened again he'd be in for it.

I remember once it was the local magistrate. He pointed out that Willy had been up before him eleven times in two years for minor traffic and other offences, and eleven times he'd had to be warned about contempt of court.

"But I'm accident-prone," interrupted Willy. "I can't help it."

"Silence!" said his Honour, banging on the bar with his little wooden knocker. "Any more of these outbursts and I'll hold you in contempt of court."

"But damn it all, Mick, you know yourself that it wasn't me who lifted them chooks. I was over at Bob's place on the Saturday and I'd have mentioned it to him if it'd been me!"

"You will address me as Your Honour," said the magistrate, banging on his bar.

"Sorry Mick," said Willy. "It was just that I was upset about being falsely accused . . ."

"I'm dismissing this charge because of insufficient evidence," said the Magistrate. "But I'm seriously considering replacing it with one of contempt. I'm not at all satisfied with your attitude towards this court."

"Thanks, Mick," said Willy. "Will you be over the club tonight?"

How Willy got away with it nobody knew. There were rumours that he was related to the magistrate through marriage but I think that was probably just an attempt to explain the unexplainable — how the hell he did it.

Another time it was Willy's boss. He'd warned Willy dozens of times that dozens of things had to stop. But Willy had dozens more little capers up his sleeve. This time it was a two-day rodeo that suddenly turned up and started being held in the boss's front paddock. It didn't take long to establish that it was the Master of Ceremonies, Willy Driver himself, who was behind it all.

There wasn't much the boss could do about it because the rodeo was to raise funds for a swimming pool for the local school and the boss had a great tribe of kids.

"I didn't actually tell them they could hold the rodeo here," explained Willy when his livid boss bailed him up about it. "I told them you'd be only too happy to help out."

Anyone else would have got the bullet right off, but, like most Hard-case Bastards, Willy was a hard man to replace on the job. Their ingenuity comes in real handy when there's any kind of emergency on. And Willy's boss knew this only too well, and what's more Willy knew his boss knew it only too well. And what's more than that, Willy's boss knew his Hard-case Bastards well enough not to have more than one of them on the payroll at any one time. Put a couple of Hard-case Bastards together and they're so busy trying to out-hard-case each other that not much work gets done, though some of the things they come up with get talked about in the district for years.

In fact many of the traditions of an area are established by the activities of Hard-case Bastards. Like the time Willy and another bloke of similar inclinations commandeered the boss's D-9 bulldozer and shoved a huge rock that marked the historic resting-place of a great Maori chief to another location 300 yards farther along the road and replaced it with an old kitchen sofa.

The main critics of Hard-case Bastards are their so-called victims, or people without much sense of humour. Like the time Willy and I had a terrific opening morning of the duck-shooting season. Limit bags, and no-one else did any good. The rumour got put around that we'd been poaching in the sanctuary, but we knew it was only because some of them were a bit sour about us having a bit of good luck and being terrifically good shots.

In fact it's worth noting that the rumour gained a great deal of momentum after the postmaster's letterbox, the glovebox of Jeff Willett's new Rambler, and Willy's boss's overcoat pockets were all found to be stuffed tight with duck feathers. (All these people, I might point out, were notoriously humourless and therefore fair game to a Hard-case Bastard.)

No, there's no doubt about the Hard-case Bastard, life would be pretty dull without him, wouldn't it?

He's the natural entertainer of this world in a way. He really enjoys entertaining other people and doesn't expect any other reward for his efforts than the delight of his audience.

Have you ever noticed that there are very few Real Hard-case Bastards in the entertainment business? Their performance seems to depend on their almost uncanny sense of what they can get away with, and it has a kind of spontaneity that you could never get through a radio or television set. They can get away with things that'd get you or I chucked out on our ears. They've got a hard-case way of telling slightly-off jokes in polite company, or putting the hard word on the host's wife and getting away with it.

I reckon we could do with more of the brand of good humour that inspires the Hard-case Bastard. He ignores the rules whenever he sees the opportunity to do so amusingly, but never deliberately hurt anybody. His ribbing seldom hurts anyone's feelings. He raves almost continuously, but you don't hear him slandering or gossiping about other people, and when somebody's in trouble the Hard-case Bastard is usually the first to come to light with a bit of practical assistance.

There's no doubt that he can become a bit tiresome or irritating at times, but when you think about it life wouldn't be the same without the imaginative carryings-on of the Hard-case Bastard.

Bless him. As a matter of fact, good reader, I can tell by the way you've been reading this that underneath it all you're a bit of a Hard-case Bastard yourself.

10
Intellectual Bastard

I MET A BRILLIANT man once. You couldn't tell he was brilliant just by looking at him, but he was. Everybody said so. He was a brilliant lecturer or architect or something.

He wasn't what you'd call a handsome man, or a well-dressed one. Nor was he particularly charming, or witty, or interesting. As a matter of fact he was bloody rude. He couldn't talk about anything or any one except himself. He interrupted conversations, ate with his mouth open and generally made everyone squirm by his sheer lack of consideration and common decency.

It didn't take me long to see that I'd run into a fully-fledged Intellectual Bastard (*Bastardus profoundus*). He was typical of them; he claimed to be an intellectual but he was really just a bastard. Half a dozen of the hundreds of obscure poems he'd written had been published in obscure literary magazines subsidised by the arts grants, so he called himself a poet.

He was phoney and ignorant, and, like all Intellectual Bastards, he protected his ignorance by assuming an air of shaky superciliousness. His intellectualness was based on such things as throwing references to obscure subjects into the conversation and leaving you stumped for words. There's not a great deal you *can* say to such things, "Of course Domingo Faustino Sarmiento in *Defence of Freedom* claims that the press is a *virtue*, rather than a collection of type-face." You either have to brave his scorn and confess that you've never head of Domingo Faustino Sarmiento, or, agree with him. Either way there's an uneasy silence because he's interrupted the flow of the conversation and the atmosphere of the gathering and it always takes a while to get going again after a thing like that happens. It's not worth trying to pin him down or prove him wrong because nearly everything he says is quoted from some musty book or other and the best you can hope for is to prove the book wrong, while he goes scot-free.

Few people speak so much and say so little as the Intellectual

Bastardus profoundus

Bastard, and they're usually talking such ephemeral, arrant nonsense that nobody could articulate about it, and the "um" and "ah" and croak and groan in between their words like somebody with a speech-impediment.

Most types of bastards are versatile enough to switch from one kind of bastardry to another, depending on the requirements of the situation, but the Intellectual Bastard is so busy maintaining his precarious perch above the rest of us that he can't let go for fear of falling in amongst us. Unthinkable! Everything he has an impulse to say must be carefully processed and worked out before he says it because the Intellectual Bastard must be absolutely correct in all he says at all times.

The result of this is that he's rarely ever right, but since he can't see it he doesn't know about it, and because he doesn't know about it it doesn't matter, because he knows everything that *does* matter.

His humour is a kind of acerbic wit that, boiled down, amounts to petty, catty, criticisms of other people. He can't fight and he can't work and he's a pacifist because he's frightened of losing his temper, and his view of that is as outrageously exaggerated as his self-importance — roughly proportionate to his *actual* importance.

As far as I'm concerned the Intellectual Bastard is a man with a great quantity of information and a great lack of knowledge. The poor bastard's the victim of the Great Academic Confidence Trick, usually worded something like, "You'll get nowhere these days without a degree behind you." And our student, hundreds of thousands of times too often, interprets this as, "I feel like I do because I haven't got a university degree. Once I get *that* everything is going to be all right. I won't feel anxious or inadequate any more. People will be nicer to me. I'll be offered jobs in high places at high salaries. Women will compete for my company. I'll be rich and famous and never have to worry about myself ever again."

And so he embarks on his chosen career of Intellectual Bastardry. After many years of study he finally graduates with the only experiences he's had during these prime years having been ones to do with studying for a university degree, and that's all the *knowledge* he can logically claim to have.

Unfortunately the only people qualified to either confirm or deny this state of affairs are those with university degrees, but by the time they've made it they're so thoroughly indoctrinated and personally committed that to explode the Academic Myth calls on them to acknowledge that their years of study and effort have been almost completely wasted. So they blindly go on supporting something that they know underneath isn't working for them, never did work for them, and probably never will work for them. This causes them to become defensive and aggressive and anxious to prove how much more than us they know — how inferior we are to them.

Perhaps the most effective way of silencing an Intellectual Bastard would be to present him with a ledger, with all he's ever *done* in one column, and the time it's taken him to do it in the other. Which goes to demonstrate that if there was any tangible way to assess the qualities of the Intellectual Bastard he wouldn't exist.

I haven't got a university degree and never had the opportunity to decide whether I wanted one or not, but I'm taking this opportunity, patient reader — Understanding Bastard (*Bastardus allknowingus*) — to tell you how pleased I am that you and I never turned out to be Intellectual Bastards.

Tash

11
Jovial Bastard

JOVIAL BASTARDS (*Bastardus jocundus*) are okay. At least they're cheerful.

Toby Mercer was about the *most* Jovial Bastard I ever met. He was so by-jovial about everything it was hard to get him to be serious. He was too big and round and bland to be anything but jovial, no matter what the circumstances were. We used to call him Ho-ho, because of him going ho-ho all the time.

"You couldn't lend me sixteen bucks, Toby," I said to him one day. "They're coming to repossess my car. I'll pay you back on payday."

"Ho-ho," said Toby. "I've only got four dollars left over from backing that double you said was going to pay a fortune last Saturday," And he slapped me on the back and told me I could borrow his pushbike to go to work on after they'd taken my car away.

Of course being a compulsory Jovialist isn't plain sailing. There were places you couldn't take Toby — funerals, for instance. I'll never forget the time I took him to my cousin's wedding. He didn't go over very well at all. Everyone got the impression that Toby was enjoying some huge joke of his own about the marriage. He and I both knew it was *their* guilty conscience. We couldn't help it if it was hard not to see that my cousin and his bride had left things a bit late in the day to get married.

The magistrate fined Toby an extra five bucks for contempt of court once. But he was really only being jovial about being fined thirty dollars for drinking after hours in the pub.

Come to think about it there were quite a few times when things would have gone much better for him if Toby had taken a more serious view of them. I remember once we were on our way back from the races at Ellerslie, broke as seven thousand bastards, and I had a go at getting a bloke in a milkbar to cash a cheque for me. I had him talked into it and was actually writing out the

62

Bastardus jocundus

cheque, when the milkbar bloke started getting uneasy about Toby grinning.

What's the joke?" he asked me, leaving my cheque on the counter.

"No joke," I said.

"Your mate seems to think so."

"Oh him," I said. "He always does that. He thinks everything's a joke. Don't you, Toby?"

"Ho-ho," said Toby, to show the milkbar bloke how jokey he thought everything was.

And as I watched him I saw the milkbar bloke go right off the idea of cashing that cheque for me.

"Sorry mate," he said, pushing the cheque back to my side of the counter as though it was infectious. "Try the bloke at the service station along here. He sometimes cashes cheques."

But of course the bloke at the service station didn't interpret Toby's ho-hoing any more accurately than the milkbar bloke had.

That night it was freezing cold and we were trying to kip down in a bus shelter when blow me down if a couple of cops in a prowl car didn't spring us. And while I was giving them our hardluck story Toby started ho-hoing again, and in the finish they got suspicious of us and took us in to the station. I could tell they were suspicious because they kept asking Toby questions about drugs. One of them seemed to have the idea that Toby was taking the micky out of him but it turned out all right in the finish. They gave us a cell to bunk down in.

If it hadn't been for Toby's ho-hoing we'd have been stuck in that bus shelter all night — but then if it hadn't been for his ho-hoing we'd have been home in bed and none of it would have happened in the first place.

It was the same the time Toby got involved in a car accident. The other bloke was indisputably in the wrong: he'd failed to stop at a compulsory stop sign and driven blindly out into the traffic, failing to give way on his right, and driven fair into the side of Toby's car. But it was Toby they took in for a blood alcohol test.

He told me later he was overjoyed that no-one had been injured and his car was covered by insurance and not even badly damaged, but the traffic officer described it as, "unnatural levity in the circumstances". It was obvious that the traffic cop didn't know about Jovial Bastards like Toby. It takes more than a minor traffic accident, or a bad day at the races, or a fine for after-hours drinking — or even a broken leg — to quell their joviality; their cheerful sense of optimism. Even so, Toby's brand of it had its drawbacks. His joviality got us the sack in the finish. We were driving trucks for a real Neurotic Bastard (*Bastardus tormentus*) of a bloke. My truck had broken a fan-belt and Toby was giving me a hand to put a new one on it, in the yard, when the boss arrived.

"What are you men doing there?" said the boss.

"Ho-ho," said Toby. "We've got a broken fan-belt. Just putting a new one on. Ho-ho."

"Who told you to do that?" demanded the boss. "Where's the mechanic?"

"Ho-ho," said Toby again. "No need to trouble him with it. We'll have it done in a couple of shakes, ho-ho."

"What's so funny about it," said the boss.

I could see that he was getting a bit strung-up about Toby saying ho-ho to him all the time. *I* mustn't laugh or he'd get really het-up — might even sack us on the spot, which we'd seen him do once or twice before — so I started grinning my head off. Couldn't help myself. Toby didn't help much, either.

"Ho-ho," he said. "It's not as serious as all that. We'll have this old tub back on the road again in no time, ho-ho."

By this time I couldn't hide my stupid grinning and the boss couldn't take it.

"Well *I* think it's very funny," he said sarcastically. "It's so bloody funny you can just ho-ho down to the office and pick up your time. Both of you!"

"Ho-ho," said Toby, as the boss got into his car and roared off.

And that was that.

It's hard for Sour Bastards (*Bastardus bitterus*) like that to believe everyone doesn't feel like they do. And, looking back on it, most of Toby's trouble was simply a matter of people not taking him at face value. They were actually suspicious of his good humour.

I often wonder where old Ho-ho is these days. It's years since I last saw him, but wherever he is and whatever he's doing, he's cheerful about it, no matter how misunderstood his joviality is.

12
Kinky Bastard

H E'S FAIRLY RARE, THE Kinky Bastard (*Bastardus loopus*). Given to playing tricks of a certain kind, often involving such things as books about sex that give you an electric shock when you open them, cushions that make unpleasant noises when you sit on them, flowers that squirt water in your face, itching powder in your sleeping bag, plastic spiders, vomits and other such delightful paraphernalia.

Kinky Bastards must be fairly widely spread because you see from the advertisements that there are people who actually manufacture and distribute this kind of gear — and, presumably, people who buy the stuff.

One Kinky Bastard on his own can usually be kept fairly harmless, but get two of them together and you've got to watch it. Three or more of them in a pack can be downright dangerous. At this point they become what is known as a Pack of Bastards. They're plain irresponsible, rather than deliberately harmful, but you have to be careful when they're about.

I knew one such Kinky Bastard who took great delight in giving people frights. He and a couple of his mates once filled a balloon with oxygen and acetylene mixture and taped it around a spark-plug of the car one of our mates was going on his honeymoon in. The couple came out of the reception with everyone waving goodbye, congratulating them, and wishing them good luck, but as soon as the groom touched the starter of the car the balloon exploded with a deafening bang and a sheet of flame. Blew the bonnet right off the car.

It was two weeks before our mate's new missus had sufficiently recovered from the shock for them to get on with their honeymoon. We knew well enough who was most likely to have done it but naturally they all denied having anything to do with it and there was nothing anyone could prove.

One of the things about Kinky Bastards is that they never learn.

Bastardus loopus

That bunch's next little trick was to pinch the toilet roll from a house we were having a party at and on their way home they ran a strip of it up the road, so that the white line curving around a bend ran on into the bank. The driver of the car that ran off the road there later that night had the usual chances of being injured or killed. As it happened the damage was slight, which was fortunate for everyone concerned.

That was when we discovered a good line of treatment for Kinky Bastards; their own medicine is an anathema to them. Some Kinky Bastard went and put a handful of sugar in the petrol-tank of their car, and another kept squirting dishwashing detergent into their jugs of beer while other Kinky Bastards diverted their attention.

And the hurt feelings of a Kinky Bastard who's had one put across him are touching to hear him complain about. The indignation, the outrage, the persecution and the sheer unfairness of it all is too heart-rending to contemplate. The suffering of a Kinky Bastard is seldom less than the very limit of human endurance.

It's hard to know what's easier to put up with — the Kinky Bastard's pranks, or his grizzling when he's on the receiving end of one of them. Even his apologies are hard to stomach.

It's not much wonder that the Kinky is one of the most studiously avoided of all Bastards. The thing that strikes me most about them is *that* they're Kinky Bastards. They're either too bored or too self-important for ordinary things to have "the desired effect" on them any more. It's got to be "way out", or "weird" or some other such thing, to appeal to their either jaded or undeveloped tastes.

They're welcome to it.

13
Lazy Bastard

ARNEY SLOAN WAS A Lazy Bastard (*Bastardus loafus*) of the first order. He was in his thirties when I met him, and in spite of the fact that he was known locally as "The Late Mr Sloan" I immediately got the unshakable impression that he was going to live for hundreds of years.

It was hard at first to believe it wasn't some kind of act he was putting on but no, it was the dinkum oil all right. He was born, bone lazy. He was so lazy he didn't even move fast enough to keep himself awake half the time, and he'd been found asleep in all sorts of unusual places.

I invited him in for a cup of tea one morning and went into the house ahead of him to get it ready. By the time I'd poured the tea Arney still hadn't come into the kitchen from the back porch, where I'd left him taking his boots off. So I had a look and found him fast asleep, sitting on the top step, leaning against the doorway, with one boot half-unlaced.

It's often true of Lazy Bastards that there's *something* they're not lazy in. Some sport, or hobby or other activity they can be encouraged to put a little bit of energy and effort into, but not so with Arney. He was a *Real* Lazy Bastard. A professional to his untrimmed fingertips. There was *nothing* he wasn't lazy about. I understand it took him four years to get through the primers at school, and by the time he left school at seventeen he'd only made it as far as form one. He wasn't dull-witted, or stupid, or unintelligent, or even careless — just lazy.

In fact it's a pretty safe bet that if Arney had been more widely-known his name would have come into the language as the perfect cliché to describe Lazy Bastards in general. (E.g. "A real *Arney Sloane* of a joker!").

He was literally too lazy to come in out of the rain. Always getting wet because he was too slow getting his coat on or getting under shelter. They'd tried to teach him to swim but had

Bastardus loafus

to give it up for fear he'd drown himself crossing the school swimming baths, for Arney a matter of endurance. And riding a bike or driving a car was absolutely out of the question for him. Neither would travel slowly enough.

Of course they'd investigated the possibility that there might be something physically wrong with Arney, but the doctors and specialists his folks consulted were unanimous. They all reported, in their discreet jargon, that he was simply a Lazy Bastard of average intelligence, ability and stature.

Arney's folks knew better than to even try sending him out to work. He just stayed on to help out round their small farm, and it says a lot of their ingenuity that they'd managed to find ways for him to be useful. For example he was an excellent gardener. He could grow anything you liked, and grow it well. It was well known that his vegetables and flowers were the best around, although many things grew a little impetuously for him at times, and he was in a constant hectic rush to keep ahead of the weeds that he was convinced sprang up behind him as soon as he turned his back. And looking at it from his pace and point of view this would be quite true of course.

His mother told me once that as a child Arney had given them no trouble whatever, too lazy to misbehave, or even get sick, I suppose. It's certainly true that he was never likely to get himself into trouble with the authorities. He was too lazy to do anything illegal, except perhaps loiter.

You may get the impression from all this that Arney was a goof, or a dope, but he wasn't. He was actually quite an interesting bloke to talk to, if you had plenty of time. He had a kind of *pace* about him that was very restful. A way of talking and moving that made you wonder what all the rush and bustle was about anyway. But I must say that after about half an hour of it you'd start getting the feeling that you hadn't had enough sleep the night before. And before you could get away from him you'd be yawning your head off. It always took me an hour or so to get myself moving properly after I'd been having a natter with Arney.

I don't know about you, dear reader — Energetic Bastard (*Bastardus whirlwindus*) — but I used to feel sorry for Lazy Bastards like Arney. Now I'm not so sure. They don't have such a hard time of it when you consider that they never get sent to fetch anything, or do anything there's any hurry to get done. And that includes just about everything in these hectic times. No one expects them to be "on time", or efficient, or stick to schedules, or even pull their weight. They just get left alone to do their own things in their own time. And yet you couldn't really call them Useless Bastards (*Bastardus nonentus*). That's a different category altogether.

Maybe they've been sent among us to remind us that we're taking things too seriously and too fast for our own good. In a world full of criticism of each other, where anything we do is liable to be wrong in *somebody's* opinion, there's few less harmful and objectionable types than the good old Lazy Bastard.

14
Miserable Bastard

YOU'VE BEEN LUCKY INDEED if you haven't run into any Miserable Bastards (*Bastardus woebegoneus*) in your time. Goodness knows, there's plenty of them around, and they never seem to go to any trouble to conceal their miserableness. Mean-ness is one of their main things, and it's a well-known fact that many well-to-do people fall into this category.

If "a man of means" means a mean man, then I think I know what it means. I mean — look at it this way, have you ever met a man of means who wasn't a mean man? Ever tried collecting money for charity? Or hitching a lift on a wet night? Not that they mean to be mean, I don't suppose, but when a man becomes a man of means he usually seems to automatically become a mean man. Or perhaps a man has to be a mean man in order to *qualify* as a man of means. Ah — to hell with it. It's no good trying to make excuses for them; it all boils down to the simple fact that they're bastards — and Miserable Bastards at that.

The Miserable Bastards I'm going to tell you about were not actually men of means, but their Miserableness was unarguable. I'd been hanging around waiting for a job at the shipyards to come up and my money was running out, so I decided to take a temporary job to tide me over. And I finally landed one in an office where they handled accounts for a big distributing outfit. Right in amongst four of the most Miserable Bastards I've ever come across.

It looked to me as though Mr Walker had been promoted to boss because nobody else would take it on. He was always busy and harrassed but you could never tell what he was actually *doing*. He was so preoccupied with things "not getting done" that he had no idea who was shirking and who was working. And when things got too far behind he'd come round complaining that he had to take the brunt. He was one of those blokes who didn't seem to have ever heard about optimism. Nothing ever went right

Bastardus woebegoneus

as far as he was concerned, and he was never more disconcerted than when he was hard-up for something or someone's inefficiency to complain about. Even the men who worked for him complained about his pessimistic view of life, and that's really saying something.

Roger, at the desk opposite mine, was iron-grey and hearty, in a miserable kind of way. He avoided as many of the monthly charge-accounts as he could and bluffed his way somehow through the rest. He was always protesting that his balance-sheets were absolutely correct, or that he hadn't been chosen to play rep. rugby for the college he went to years before.

He seemed to be married but went out of his way to be a bachelor in front of the girls in the outer office. One of them was always on the very verge of cracking him one every time he lechered around her, but Roger didn't seem to be aware of the effect he had on her, or anyone else, for that matter.

Alex, in the far corner of the office, was leathery, lined and leaning, with an aggressive misleading handshake and as miserable a disposition as it's ever been my misfortune to be confined in the same office with. He wore tight collars, chain-smoked, and had been forced to give up his own business because of bad health. He kept bottles of pills in his pockets and desk drawers and was full of endless misinformation about the political situation.

I was a bit chary of Alex, and it seemed to be mutual. Whenever I approached his desk he hastily covered whatever he was doing with papers and books, as though the Overdue Accounts he dealt with were highly classified information. It was rumoured that Alex took his wife's false teeth to work with him in case she ate too much while he was away. He was such a Miserable Bastard he'd pretend not to have noticed you arrive, rather than spend a "Good morning" on you.

Harold fretted nervously over "Discounts and Refunds" at the desk opposite Alex. He was petulant and never to blame, and he'd probably caught his severe miserableness from the environment he worked in as though it was a rampant virus. He was always shifting his weightless support back and forth between Roger's and Alex's phoney lack of antagonism towards one another. He distrusted me because I wouldn't take sides in his one-sided, unspoken quarrels with the rest of them.

Most of the work in the place was finally put together and concluded by Walker's secretary, Mrs Smith, the only one I liked in the whole outfit. But she didn't like me and we hardly ever spoke to one another.

Mrs Smith had been there for uncountable years and during the changes of staff she'd survived she'd had to learn and teach every different job in the office and she was the only one who actually understood how it all worked. I don't think she had any idea that she was the key figure in the whole business. None of them were likely to tell her, either, the miserable bastards.

I stuck it out for two weeks, an eternity, and as soon as old Walker had been round with my first pay-envelope I suddenly decided to leave before the atmosphere of misery and complaint infected me beyond recovery. But I just couldn't walk out without saying goodbye to Roger, Alex and Harold.

So I put everything that was mine into my pockets and went over to where Harold was shuffling through papers as though he'd just lost one of them.

"Here, Harold," I said, slipping him a folded dollar note I'd got ready. "You'd better put this towards it. I'm sorry I can't make it a bit more, but I've had to pay him not to report *me*."

Harold was so taken by surprise that he took the money, and I could see that there was no need for me to say anything else because he'd gone as white as a dismissal-notice. So I nodded understandingly, patted him on the shoulder, and went across to Alex, who shuffled the letter he was writing under some papers on his desk and gave me a hostile look.

"What do you want?" he said. "You'll get us all into trouble if Walker comes in — hanging around the desks like this."

I bent down so close to his ear that he nearly fell off his chair trying to get further away from me.

"You'd better get onto him before he takes this thing any further," I whispered urgently.

"Who! Who! What are you talking about?" he whispered back. And he started shooting quick, nervous glances around the office as though he'd just heard someone was sneaking up on him.

"I'll try and back you up, of course," I whispered, "but it'll cost you hundreds if it ever gets as far as the courts."

And before he could say anything else I left him and went across to Roger, who'd seen that something was going on and had his hearty guilt ready to receive me.

"What's wrong with Alex," he said. "Looks as though he's been caught cooking the books," he joked nervously.

And on the spur of the moment I took him up on it. "I'd be very careful about spreading these rumours, if I were you, Mr Samson," I warned him severely. "Nothing is going to be decided until my report has been considered by the board."

That set him back on his miserable heels better than anything I could have thought up without his help.

"You mean you're from . . ." he stammered. "You've been . . ."

"I'm not in a position to say any more, at this juncture," I interrupted him. "And I strongly advise you to keep the whole matter entirely to yourself."

"Well you won't find anything wrong with *my* books," he blustered guiltily.

"That remains to be seen," I said.

And I left the office, ignoring Alex's nervous jerking and hissing for me to come over to his desk and tell him "who" and "what".

"That should give them something to be miserable about," I said to Mrs Smith on my way past her desk and out into the street.

And I wasn't even tempted to go back and see what happened to The Miserable Bastards.

15

Nasty Bastard

WE ALL KNOW HIM. He infests every stratum of our over-loaded society, and he spreads treachery and deception wherever he goes amongst us.

I speak of course, of the Nasty Bastard (*Bastardus notquiteniceus*). The kind of bastard who doesn't know how to be honourable or honest. He doesn't lie and cheat by accident, or to protect anyone else's feelings, or to get himself out of trouble, he does it automatically, without regard for the consequences to himself or anyone else.

One of the unfortunate characteristics of the Nasty Bastard is that he's always on the move, spreading his maliciousness far and wide. This is mainly because his activities start catching up on him after a while and rather than permit himself to be confronted by the truth or face the consequences of his deceptions he takes to his miserable scrapers and sets himself up in his troublous practices somewhere else.

Bertie (the germ) Bell was a Nasty Bastard, and, as with most of his kind, he had the knack of taking people in at first. On acquaintance, even if somebody warned you about him, you were impressed by his worldliness and his adroit knack of flattery; his unconcerned attitude towards money (although he never seemed to actually *have* any). But it wouldn't be long before his true colours emerged. At the first opportunity he'd bounce one of his rubber cheques on you, or — even worse — he'd get you to bounce one on someone else for him, and in such a way there wouldn't be much you could do about it.

Bertie used to hang around the periphery of our group, not being either welcome or qualified to join us. He was the sort of bastard you had to be downright rude to before you could get rid of him. And nobody liked to do that because they knew it'd spoil the atmosphere of the party or drinking-school they were in. He'd make strong men furious with themselves for having

Bastardus notquiteniceus

to cross streets or make excuses of previous engagements in order to avoid his unpleasant company.

Occasionally some misguided soul would take pity on little Bertie and try to be friends with him. This always had the effect of causing Bertie to despise them and they inevitably suffered for their pains. He'd either steal from them, try to get them to steal *for* him, or cause trouble between them and the rest of their friends. So the aim was to avoid Bertie and, temporarily, anyone who was with him. He was too much a Nasty Bastard.

He cheated at games. He stole small change. He passed detrimental information, often *false* information, back and forth between friends and groups. He stole whenever there was an opportunity combined with a good chance of his getting away with it or blaming someone else. He'd start fights and if he couldn't avoid getting involved in them it'd be Bertie who'd use a bottle or a broken glass on someone who was already down. Then he would swear it was somebody else.

Like most Nasty Bastards, Bertie wasn't unknown to the police by any means. It was well known that he had an unenviable list of convictions for crimes involving double-dealing, fiddling, petty-theft, shoplifting, consorting, drug-possession, cashing dud cheques, and other such shabby and wretched offences. And it was less well-known that he was suspected in some circles of being a police-informer, and rumour had it that he was only at large because of the useful information he passed on to the authorities about the criminal scene. So that law-abiding citizens and criminals (and those in-between) all avoided Bertie as though he was a rampant plague all of his own.

Bertie was a journalist and specialised in ferreting out stories of sordid interest for Sunday newspapers. The kind of story that is damaging to the names and reputations of those involved, without making any difference to the world at large. Things like divorce and adultery, sex crimes, and details of perverse and other unsavoury offences — these were the tools of Bertie's unwholesome trade.

And if that's not a Nasty Bastard I don't know what is.

The last I heard of Bertie he was in trouble with a private detective agency. Apparently they'd recruited him to play the part

81

of "the other man" in a jacked-up divorce case. They paid him half the money and told him when and where to report for duty. But while he and the woman were waiting in the motel unit to be caught in compromising circumstances by the people from the private detective agency Bertie decided to take advantage of the situation — no one could be expected to believe he was being something so un-nasty as conscientious — and the result of it was that when the rest of them got there all hell was in the process of breaking loose. The woman was tearing around half-dressed in the motel car-park, yelling out that she was being raped, while Bertie was in the office trying to get them to ring a taxi for him.

They managed to keep the police out of it, but the divorce thing was a complete wash-out. And Bertie only escaped a charge of indecent assault because of his unhesitating willingness to expose the whole bunch of them. They even had to pay him the other half of his fee to try and keep him quiet about it, but this wasn't at all successful. Bertie couldn't wait to tell everybody he met. In fact if the story hadn't been verified by a mate of ours whose brother-in-law runs the motel where it happened none of us would have believed a word of it.

And all that was only a couple of months ago so it looks as though if Bertie is ever going to change for the better it won't be for a while yet.

16
Officious Bastard

YOU FIND HIM IN GOVERNMENT Departments and in the lower gears of business-corporation coggery. He usually asks you if he can help you in a way that leaves you in no doubt that you've got yourself embroiled in the starchy, ritualistic caution of the Officious Bastard (*Bastardus correctus*). And the very presence of one of the Officious Bastards is enough to reduce the average Unruffable Bastard (*Bastardus coolus*) to jibbering obsequiousness.

I went one day to get the electricity turned on in a flat I'd just rented and ran into it head-on. I'd been waiting around in the big glass electricity building just long enough for the atmosphere to un-nerve me when I saw one of them moving towards me. Slow and preoccupied, like a man who's just been told he hasn't long to live and can't work out how to put in the rest of his time. He came right up to me and just as I thought he was going right past he suddenly acknowledged that he'd seen me. He said.

"Can I help you, sir?"

And like a fool, not knowing whether he could help me or not, I said, "Yes." And then I added, "I'd like to get the power put on."

"I see," he said. But he said it very slowly and cautiously, as though I'd told him I wanted to test a nuclear device in the basement of the Power Board Building and he'd never had to deal with such a request before. And then, after a thoughtful pause, he said, "What address?"

I told him the address.

"Are you the consumer?" he asked me.

"Have you filled in your application form?" he asked me.

"No," I said. "I haven't."

"Well you'll have to fill one of those in," he said. "They're on the desk over there."

So I went and got one of their application forms and filled it

Bastardus correctus

Bastardus correctus,

in. Name, address, how long I'd been there, previous address, how long I'd been *there* — etc. etc., and then I had to wait to get to see the same Officious Bastard again. He went through the application form and then told me to wait and went off somewhere.

There's an uneasy guilty feeling when an Officious Bastard takes a form you've just filled with information about yourself and goes off to check it, but this one didn't keep me long. He was back in about five minutes and I could see by the way he approached that something had been decided or resolved.

"Would you come through please," he said to me. "The Credit Manager would like a word with you."

So I followed him into the glassy-eyed office of his Credit Manager, who sat behind a desk that was bare except for my application form.

"Sit down, Mr — er — Mumble," he said. "You're the new tenant of this — er — flat," he accused me, checking everything he said against the incriminating information on the application form.

"Yes," I confessed.

"I see," he said. "We've had a lot of trouble with the previous tenants of this particular property, Mr — er — Clamp. There's still an outstanding account owing for electricity from last May and June."

"I don't know anything about that," I told him. "I just want the power turned on."

"I see," he said. "Well we'll have to get a deposit of six dollars from you. A guarantee, you understand."

"That's okay," I said, getting my wallet out. "When can you turn the power on?"

"There'll be a re-connection fee of two dollars, fifty," he went on. "We had to disconnect the supply for non-payment of the account."

"Here you are then," I said, and offered him ten dollars to show him I had money.

"You'll have to pay the cashier in the outer office," he said.

"Oh," I said. "All right then, I'll do that. Is there anything else you want from me?"

"I think that'll be all, thank you," he said. "I'll hand your application on to the Service Department."

"When will my power be turned on?" I asked him.

"Oh — it should be on by tomorrow," he said.

"But what am I going to do tonight!" I said.

"Well, you *have* left it a little late in the day," he said doubtfully, looking at his watch. "All the vehicles will be out on the road by this time. We're very busy just now," he added.

"But I've just moved in," I said. "I haven't even unpacked, and I've only got today off work. There's no hot water or anything."

"We can't help that, Mr — er — Clump. You should have come in earlier."

"But I *couldn't* get in any earlier," I said desperately. "Isn't there anything you can do to hurry it up?"

And suddenly I saw that this particular Officious Bastard had got what he wanted. I was grovelling. He was now prepared to exert his authority on my behalf.

"Well in that case," he said magniloquently, "I'll see what I can do for you. I won't promise anything, mind, but I may be able to have a word with the head of our Service Department."

I was overwhelmed. This bureaucratic dignitary was actually going to pull strings for me; use his far-reaching influence and sway to get the power on for me; bring into play his power-behind-the-throne of the Electricity Department, just so I could have electric light and hot water; plug in my humble electric jug and have a cup of tea — even cook myself sausages and eggs on the electric stove.

Because of this Officious Bastard's great prestige and influence in Power Board circles I needn't after all go to work without my breakfast in the morning. I was benumbed and the humble gratitude I expressed to him embarrasses me still whenever I think about it.

And imagine my feelings on arriving back at my new flat and seeing the power-board truck parked outside.

"That's pretty quick work," I said admiringly to the three electricity men who were even then putting the plug back in, or whatever they have to do to justify the reconnection fee.

"What do you mean, quick work?" said one of the men defensively (I think he thought I was being sarcastic).

"I've only just come from the Power Board Office," I told him. "I thought I'd be lucky to get the power connected at all today."

"Oh, there's nothing much on today," he said. "They just called us up on the R.T. . . . There y'are," he added, closing the junction-box or whatever it was, "You're connected!"

And, sure enough, when I went inside and switched on the nearest electric light — it worked! I had the power on.

But I couldn't shake the feeling that in spite of their efficiency the Officious Bastards at the Power Board Office had put one over on me, which happens every time I encounter them. I wonder if there's something psychologically wrong with me?

17

Poor Bastard

APOSSUM-MAN IS LIKE a possum dog. They're a special kind of people. When the price of the skins drops away to barely worthwhile and doesn't look like it'll ever pick up again, and all the money-hunters quit the game, and there's rumours of synthetic fibres taking over from the possum skin, the genuine possum-man will keep on going; running out his lines and accumulating racks and bundles of beautifully-done skins to send away to the dwindling market. And strangely enough it's never dwindled away completely. They've always managed to keep going.

Except for their loyalty to the profession, there's nothing to distinguish one possum-man from another. I've seen them short and thin, short and stocky, long and beefy, long and thin — but most of them are old-timers. A possum-man who can't remember when you used to have to have a licence to trap them, and a government tag on each skin you sold, is a newcomer to the game. They usually work alone because no two of them will ever agree on the same best areas and methods to get the best possum skins. You still run across the odd possum-man in out-of-the-way pubs, or pass him on the road when you're taking a short cut through some back way or other. You can tell him by his dog, if his vehicle or his appearance don't give him away.

But this yarn isn't about possum-men, I only mentioned them to remind you about them. In fact this yarn is about the only exception to the above rule I ever knew. His name was Cecil Groson and he should have been one of the best possum-men in the game. He'd had plenty of opportunity to be, goodness knows. His old man was one of the oldest of the oldtimers, and still going strong when I knew Cecil. But the trouble was that Ces was an incurable Poor Bastard (*Bastardus upagainstitus*).

I met his old man once or twice. He was trapping on a Maori block in the Urewera and he was camped in a hut I used to use

Bastardus upagainstitus

sometimes, half an hour in from the Wairoa Road. He was a bloody good trapper, old Claude Groson, there was no doubt about that. And he'd talk to you about possums and the bush and the seasons and the spread of the opossum across the country since they were first released here in 1866 — but he wouldn't talk about Cecil. At the very mention of Cecil's name the old man's mouth would shut like a sprung trap and nothing would get him going again until next time you saw him.

You couldn't blame the old man in a way. Cecil must have been a great disappointment to him — he was everything the old man wasn't, and nothing that he was. The only thing in Cecil's favour was that he never gave up trying — and a lot of people would have told you that wasn't *in* his favour, if you'd asked them.

There were two impressive things about Cecil Groson. The first was his appearance. He was tall and lean, and straight and bent forward slightly from the hips like a man who's been used to carrying heavy loads all his life. He had a long hooked nose and his long straight mouth curled downward at the corners. His eyes were round and dark, and his eyebrows curved across his receding forehead like the wings of a descending hawk. No humour there, you'd swear to look at him. Not a man to tamper with you'd say to yourself or your closest mate. But then he'd open his mouth, and that was the other impressive thing about him.

It wasn't that all the top teeth were missing from one side of his mouth and most of the bottom ones from the other side. It wasn't that you could suddenly see that the turned-down mouth was really an upside-down grin (and a pretty stupid-looking grin at that). No, it wasn't the deception of his appearance, or the unexpectedly high-pitched giggle and whine of his voice, or even the slightly ridiculous way he said the slightly ridiculous things he did. It was a kind of *atmosphere* the man had. Hard to put your finger on, but it was impressive all right, you can take my word for that. The nearest anyone ever got to summing it up was probably when my old mate Clive Piper remarked just after Ces had left the pub in quest of another disaster one day — "A bit of a *Poor* Bastard, old Ces."

The only reason a few of us used to let Ces pretend to be a

90

mate of ours was because we felt kind of sorry for him. Whenever you ran into him he'd have just done something bad. I remember once it was forgetting to hang up the phone properly after he'd rung long-distance, and whacked up a colossal toll account for the bloke whose telephone he was using. Another time he'd got caught in the rain with a thousand first-grade possum skins on a packhorse and nothing to cover them with. Three months' work down the drain. And then there was the time we ran into him in the pub and he'd just poisoned nineteen sheep the night before.

Not that we were particularly surprised to hear about that because Ces had a reputation with cyanide. He'd poisoned things nobody knew you *could* poison with it. Things like goats, and birds, a horse — and once, he swears, an eel, two hundred yards from the nearest creek. He poisoned stoats, polecats, hedgehogs, rabbits, earthworms, pigs, a stag, rats, his dog, and quite a few possums as well.

At first we used to think he was being dogged with his usual run of bad luck, but it was a bit too much even for that. And then we found out why. A bunch of the boys were out pig-hunting and they came across a cyanide line Cecil had laid the day before. And what a line! It was an almost continuous trail of potassium cyanide and flour, right across the watershed. He'd plastered the stuff everywhere. Must have used pounds and pounds of it. The boys doubled back and went round to Cecil's camp to see what he was up to, and there he was. Grinding up big hunks of cyanide out of a tin — with an ordinary meat-mincer — on the table inside his hut. How he hadn't poisoned himself with it no-one could understand.

Nobody would let Ces lay cyanide on their property after that, so he went back to running equally ruinous trap-lines though they weren't so potentially dangerous as the cyanide.

I don't know about the other blokes, but Ces used to make me feel so sorry for him that I couldn't stand the sight of him for more than a few minutes at a time. Not that he used to complain, mind you. He'd cheerfully tell you about his most recent disaster and then he'd go on, just as cheerfully, to tell you about the next catastrophe he was planning. You just *knew* he was going to make a dismal balls-up of it, whatever it was.

By conscientiously going from one cheerful calamity to the next, Ces eventually worked his way out of the district, and you'd only run into him occasionally when you were on your way to or from somewhere else. But it was enough to keep you advised that he hadn't changed much.

I never saw him for about four years at one stage. And the next time I did see him it was to be the last, though of course I didn't know that till much later on. I'd heard the odd report that he was working in the Waioeka Gorge area — on possums, but that was all, until I was passing through there one day and pulled over to the edge of the road to let an old jalopy get past. There'd been a slip. The road was pretty narrow and windy and steep around there and the other vehicle didn't look as though it was particularly strong on brakes. And who do you think was driving it. . . ?

Yes, it was Ces. Same as ever. We sat there yarning through the windows of our vehicles until a Public Works truck came along and we had to shift to let it get past.

"Turn around and follow me!" shouted Ces as he moved off. "I'm camped just down here a bit."And he drove away, waving out the window of his bomb to the blokes in the P.W. truck.

Well I had a perfect opportunity to avoid Ces that time. All I had to do was just keep going. But somehow I didn't like to. He was so pleased to see me, and, besides, I'd had a fair spell without him. I felt I could stand a little more. So I found a place to turn round and drove back. Ces was waiting for me where a track turned off the road and followed a small creek up into the bush. The track got rougher and rougher and just before it became impossible to go any further, we came to Ces's camp. It was a broken-down old hut with possum-boards leaning all around the outside walls. He had his dried skins hanging in bundles in a lean-to at the back of the hut and she stank a fair bit, but apart from that it wasn't a bad camp. For Ces.

He stoked up the fire, chattering all the time like someone who's had nobody to talk to for a long time, and we had a brew of tea in filthy mugs. He'd been there for six weeks, in this particular area, and it was the best place he'd ever struck. Never been trapped before. Of course he'd had one or two minor set-backs

— like having sixty traps pinched off the back of his waggon, and nearly having to go back to using cyanide. But, fortunately, he'd got another fifty traps on credit so he was able to keep going without using poison. And, as I say, it was just as bloody well.

I won't explain how it came about, but I ended up agreeing to stay the night. Ces knew this place out on a farm at the edge of the bush that was absolutely crawling with possums. We were going out there for a bit of sport that night. He had a big hand-spotlight with a practically brand-new battery he'd been saving for an occasion like this. He was to spotlight the possums and I was to shoot them out of the trees, in their hundreds, with his old .22 rifle. And just to make sure of any wounded ones, we took Ces's new possum-dog with us. A fair-dinkum cracker-jack possum-dog he reckoned. Best one he'd ever had. Looking at the dog, and knowing Ces, I had my doubts about it, but as long as he was happy it didn't make any difference whether the dog was no better than any of the one's he'd had when he was down our way.

Now it wasn't that I should have known better than to get myself involved in one of Ces's capers — I *did* know better. And I didn't like the idea of it any the more for that. But, as I said, he was so pleased to see one of the "old mates", and it was me who was handling the rifle. I couldn't see what could go wrong, but that didn't make much difference either. No one had ever been able to foresee any of Ces's disasters. So I wasn't all that terribly optimistic when we pulled up in his truck, about an hour after dark, at this place where Ces reckoned all the possums were.

And I'll tell you what — there were possums there all right! We lit up fifteen or twenty of them with Ces's big torch before we even got into the paddock. They were perched all over the trees and scattered everywhere across the grass out from the bush edge. I didn't get much of a chance for a decent look around because Ces took one sweep with the light and then he and his dog were through the fence and off down the hill, with Ces hissing, "There they are! Come on!", with his spotlight waving around like a crashing car, leaving me to try and finish loading the rifle in the dark.

I caught up with him about halfway down the slope. He had

three possums lit up in a dead popular and he was just about climbing up the beam of his spotlight to get at them.

"Here they are! Here they are!" he hissed at me. "Shoot the little bastards! Hurry up! Shoot! Shoot!"

So I shot. Got two of them, and hit the branch beside the third, and it ran down the tree and jumped out onto the grass at the other side of the trunk. Ces immediately gave chase, yelling to his dog to "Skitchem!", but his dog was busy shaking the fur out of one of the dead possums and didn't seem to hear him. So Ces took off across the paddock trying to keep his light on the possum that was scampering across the ground in front of him.

And suddenly there was this almight crashy and Ces's torch flew through the air like a Catherine-wheel and landed a bit further down the hill and went out on the third bounce.

By the time I got there my eyes were adjusting to the darkness and I could see what had happened. The possum had shot straight under a seven-wire fence and Ces hadn't even seen it coming. He'd cannoned into it at full tilt and bounced about twelve feet back into the paddock. After a while I got him sitting up and explained what had happened to him. And as soon as he could move he crawled off along the fence looking for his light. He found it just through the fence about ten yards down the hill and as soon as he picked it up it flickered on. And it flickered on and off all the time after that.

I wanted to call it a night and get back to the camp, but Ces wouldn't hear of it. We'd come out to shoot possums, and shoot possums we would. So I gave in and we set off again, along the bush edge, with Ces limping badly and bumping his torch on and off and trying not to grunt from the pain of his injuries. At least he wasn't going to go dashing off after any more possums. Not that night, anyway.

We got another four of five possums but with the light going on and off all the time it was a bit awkward and I'd just got Ces talked into working our way back towards where we'd left the truck when he spotted a big buck possum perched in the top of a small punga. He kept the spotlight on-and-off it while I moved in for a shot, and just as I was getting into position, several things happened . . .

94

First, the possum jumped out of the punga. Secondly, Ces's torch went out. Thirdly, Ces's dog headed the possum off. Fourthly, the possum saw Ces standing there and thought he was a stump and ran up him to get away from the dog, and perched there on Ces's head, with its claws dug into his face and scalp. Fifthly, Ces dropped the torch, and it came on and illuminated . . . Sixthly, Ces's dog jumped up and, Oh God, was dragging the possum off Ces's head.

As soon as I picked up the torch it went out again, and when I joggled it on and saw Ces's face I tried to quickly joggle it out again, but it stayed on. What a mess! For a start he was covered in blood. One of his ear lobes was split nearly right through, and his face was ripped in several deep ragged lines from his forehead to his chin.

Ces's dog yelped in pain somewhere out across the paddock and a few minutes later he came back. That possum must have been a bit too much for him.

Ces was vaguely trying to smear the blood off his face with the sleeve of his woollen jersey and I waited to hear from him so I could tell exactly how badly hurt he was. It looked like a hospital job to me.

Then Ces spoke, "William Tell would have shot that possum right off my head," he said, grinning through the blood.

He was a hospital job all right, but not the kind of hospital I'd first had in mind. Poor Bastard.

I got him back to the truck. I got him back to camp. I got him cleaned up and sticking-plastered and bandaged. I got him into his bunk and gave him a brew of tea. And I got the hell out of there at first light the next morning.

The next I heard of Ces was when one of the blokes found him in the obituary column and brought the cutting into the pub:

GROSON, CECIL EDWARD. Accidentally, at Waioeka Gorge. Son of Claude and Emily. Brother of Jane. Sadly missed.

And it gave the date, just three weeks after I'd last seen him, after the night of the possums.

I got to wondering about it. After all the disasters and catastrophes and calamities and things Ces had survived it was hard

95

to imagine what kind of mere accident could have carried him off. I remembered him waving to the blokes in the Public Works truck the day I met him in the gorge, and when I was up that way a couple of weeks later I ran into a bunch of them clearing a slip off the road. So I stopped and asked them if they knew Ces Groson.

They knew him all right. They knew he was dead, too. They even knew one of the blokes who found him. And, yes, they knew how it happened.

It seems that the Public Works blokes used to drop Ces off a couple of loaves of bread two or three times a week, and when they found that he wasn't collecting it two of them went up to his camp to see if he was okay. His dog was there but there was no sign of Ces. And it didn't look as though the camp had been used for a few days. So they reported him missing and the police and a few of the locals got up a search party.

They split up into two groups and went looking for him. One lot found his trap line. No possums and every trap sprung. Only Ces would have done that. Then the other party found Ces. He wasn't hard to locate. You see, they came across this dirty great cyanide-line, running right through the bush. Cyanide everywhere. They followed it along and found dead wekas, and possums, dead rats . . . and where the line ended they found Ces. Dead. from cyanide. He'd finally rounded off his tally. The variety of kills he made with the potassium cyanide must surely and post-humously, be a record for Ces Groson. Poor old Ces. Sadly missed. You get blokes like that. Poor bastards.

18

Queer Bastard

THE OLD MEANING OF this description of a bastard is long since outdated. In other words, there's nothing queer about queers these days.

No, the Queer Bastard (*Bastardus quaintus*) as we know him today is one who is not quite the full quid, but more peculiar than mad. Whimsical, perhaps, even a little faddy or weird. Possibly even dotty, potty, batty, dippy, dizzy, giddy, screwy, wacky; scatty or daft. But definitely not nuts or crackers. That is, if my old mate Clive Piper is anything to go by. And if *he* wasn't a Queer Bastard nobody was.

Clive was so strange he was often taken for a lunatic at first sight or acquaintance, but once you got to know him you realised that there was a kind of logic to what he did and said. Like the time I was fifty yards from the post office when I noticed that the letter he'd asked me to post for him was addressed to Ho Chi Minh in North Vietnam. I didn't want him getting himself into trouble so I took the letter back to Clive's place to see if he'd like to change his mind about it, and found him taking all the windows out of his house.

"What are you doing there, Clive?" I asked him.

"I'm taking all my windows out," he said.

"What are you doing that for?" I asked him.

"To turn them round — end for end," he said.

"Why?" I said.

"Because they've been up this way for forty years," he said.

"What's the difference?" I said.

"Don't you know about glass?" he asked me.

"What about it?"

"It's liquid," he explained.

"Liquid?"

"Yes," he said. "The glass at the bottom of all these windows is thicker than the glass at the top because they've been up this

Bastardus quaintus

way all the time. I'm turning them round so they'll last longer. Otherwise they'll get too thin at the top and break when I go to clean them."

"What about this letter?" I said to change the subject.

"What about it?"

"It's addressed to Ho Chi Minh," I said. "In North Vietnam."

"So it should be," he said. "That's who it's written to."

"You mean you've actually written a letter to Ho Chi Minh?" I said.

"You've got it in your hand," he pointed out. "I thought you were going to post it for me."

"I will," I said. "I was just wondering why you'd want to write to Ho Chi Minh, that's all."

"It's personal," he said.

So I gave up. Posted his letter and tried to forget about it, but I couldn't forget about him turning all his windows upside-down. I was worried that my old friend might be finally slipping off the wrong side of the wall he'd been balancing on for so long. So I checked up, and you know what I found?

I found that glass *is* a liquid and is never anything else. And that the glass at the bottom of Clive's windows was, after forty years, undoubtedly thicker than the glass at the top. There was some doubt about the efficacy of turning windows upside-down to make them less likely to break, but I wasn't going to argue about that. Clive was okay after all. His old abnormal self.

I went round to his place, almost a month since I'd last seen him, to agree with him about the windows, and found him up on the roof, sweeping it with a straw broom.

"What are you up to, Clive?" I called up to him.

"Sweeping the roof," he called back.

"What are you sweeping the roof for?"

"Because it's dirty," he called down to me. "It gets all the stuff from the factories around here on it. I sweep it every three months or so."

"What's the difference?" I called up.

"The paint lasts three times as long if you sweep it occasionally," he said. "There's a lot of chemicals in that stuff."

"What about the rain," I tried. "Doesn't that wash it off?"

"The paint lasts three times as long if you sweep it down every three months or so," he repeated.

So I waited for him to finish sweeping his roof and when he came down we had a cup of tea.

"Did you get a reply from Ho Chi Minh?" I asked him casually.

"Yes," he said. "It came just yesterday, as a matter of fact."

"What did it say?" I asked sceptically.

"That's personal," he said.

"Did you save the postage stamps on the envelope?" I asked him cunningly.

"The envelope's still on the dresser there. You can have the stamps if you want them."

And, sure enough, he produced the letter he'd got from Ho Chi Minh and let me tear the North Vietnamese stamps off the North Vietnamese envelope. All he would tell me was that some people demonstrate, some people raise funds, others write letters to the newspapers, and he writes to Ho Chi Minh. I'd have given anything to find out what was in that letter, but I never did.

"What sort of a bloke is he to write to?" I asked as a last resort.

"Better than the other joker," said Clive. "*He* didn't even reply to my letter himself. He got someone else to do it for him."

"What other joker's that?" I asked him.

"President Nixon," said Clive. "The stamps off his letters are still around somewhere if you want them."

"No thanks," I stammered. "It doesn't matter any more."

And Clive looked at me kind of thoughtful for a moment or two, and then, "Y'know," he said. "you're a bit of a *Queer* Bastard at times."

"Me? Queer!" I said to him.

"Yes," he said.

"How do you work that out?" I said, settling down to hear him get himself into the usual entertaining tangle.

"You waste time all the time," he said.

"I don't get you," I said.

"Every time you ask me something I tell you — then you ask me again, and I tell you again — then you check up on it later to see if I was putting you crook or not. And I've never put you crook yet, so that means you've wasted all the time you've spent

100

checking up on me so far, and you're *still* doing it. You still haven't found out that it's easier to believe what someone tells you and maybe come a gutser every once in a while, than to make sure everything's dead right before you can accept it.

"And if *that*," concluded Clive. "isn't a Queer Bastard, I don't know what is."

Me neither. If that's the kind of queerness Clive's been writing to people like Ho Chi Minh and President Nixon about I can only hope it had the effect on them that it did on me.

19
Rude Bastard

DON'T LET'S RUN AWAY with the erroneous notion that Rude Bastards (*Bastardus badmannerus*) are ignorant. They not only know about manners and how to use them, they believe in them — providing they don't have to use them themselves. In fact there's nobody more likely to be indignant about the lack of manners than a Rude Bastard.

You'd expect Rude Bastards to be almost exclusively confined to us lower classes, the proletarians, the workers. But I want to bring your attention to the lawyer who makes an appointment with you and then abruptly breaks off discussing your affairs to talk on his telephone for endless minutes, consulting files and making notes, while you sit there like some intruder, wondering what it's going to cost you. These men have secretaries and receptionists to take their telephone calls and tell the callers to ring later, but they're not instructed to do this because Mr Lawyer has his spatulate fingers in so many trust-account pies that he can't afford to attend to one thing at a time any longer. There's a *Real* Rude Bastard for you.

And then there's the doctor who, before you've finished telling him your symptoms, drags his prescription-pad across, scribbles something like the tracks of a drunken fowl on it, hands it to you and tells you to see the nurse on your way out to make an appointment for another dose of the same ignorance.

I don't give a damn how overworked they are. They're well-paid for every patient they're off-hand with. If you or I started skimping our work in that manner simply because we had a lot of it to do we'd be out of our jobs pretty smartly. And a physician who refused to discuss your health with you when you consult him about it is nothing but a Rude Bastard, in anybody's language.

And what about the Magistrate who takes advantage of his position in the intimidating environs of one of *our* courtrooms

Bastardus badmannerus

to make his ill-mannered, corny and sarcastic personal remarks about the character of his victims? As Rude a Bastard as you can get.

The psychologist we're invited to go to for help, only to be told something ludicrous like, "You have a deep-seated personality defect." He's a bloody jargoneer — another Rude Bastard.

The television interviewer who invites an expert to tell the viewers about something he has a specialised knowledge of, and then proceeds to question the veracity of the expert's information in order to gain for himself a reputation for hard-hitting interviewing. A Rude Bastard.

Officialdom, too, has a goodly share of Rude Bastards in its ranks. And personally I've had a gutful of it. The next so-called professional man, official, honorary ranger, policeman, traffic officer, receptionist, or anyone else who has me in a position where I need something from him, and takes advantage of it to exercise his native rudeness, is going to find out that I can be a pretty Rude Bastard myself. And, unlike him, I will have the advantage of being able to help it.

I cordially invite you, mannerly reader, to join the Society For The Giving Of Just Deserts To Rude Bastards, which you can become a life member of by simply informing the next Rude Bastard you run into that you object to his, or her, lack of manners. They'll know what you mean. Good luck!

20
Situational Bastard

BASTARDRY IS NOT RESTRICTED to cataloguing types of people. A man can get himself into a bastard of a situation, for instance, if he doesn't watch it. And I can't think of a better example of this than the time I got collared to look after my sister's kids for a couple of hours while she was getting her teeth fixed up.

There were two of them, both girls, and I didn't know them very well in those days. The oldest was about belt-high and the other one wasn't different enough so I could tell which was Lucy and which was May.

I was a bit out of my depth at the kid-minding caper, but I reckoned the best thing to do was take them into town and buy them something. They seemed to think it was a fair enough idea and they got into the car without any persuading. And off we went, with the two kids jumping all over the seats, nattering like sparrows and asking me all kinds of crazy questions. Apart from that everything was going off okay, but before we got to town they suddenly decided they wanted to go to the toilet. First one of the them, and then the other.

And by the time we'd got to town it was getting urgent — for all of us. They were jumping from foot to foot, hanging onto themselves, crossing their legs, and generally carrying on something terrible.

I was a bit stonkered. I thought of asking some woman to help us out but none of the ones I saw along the streets looked as though they'd have been very approachable on the subject. And then I thought about the student building at the university. I remembered it from the time I was trotting a woman who took lectures there. And the toilets were just inside the main door.

I pulled up outside the place, just in time, by the way the kids were performing, and took them in. There was no one around just then but it didn't make any difference. I opened the door

Bastardus setuppus

of the women's outfit for them and saw that there was another door for them to get through, but they managed to shove it open. It sprung shut behind them and I stood around waiting.

They took a hell of a long time in there and I was thinking of asking the next woman who came past if she'd mind checking up on them for me. Then I heard the youngest one half-crying inside the toilet and woke up to what was happening. That inside door was too tough for them to pull open and they were stuck in there.

And I'd just opened the outside door to go in and let them out when someone came down some stairs behind me and a woman's voice said, "Hey there! What do you think you're doing!"

So I let the door shut again and said to her, "It's okay, lady. I'm just going in here to get a couple of young girls."

"You're doing no such thing," she said. "Get away from there at once!"

And before I could explain, there were people coming from all directions until I was surrounded by them. And that woman was telling everyone in a loud voice how she'd caught me in the very act of breaking into the women's toilet to get at some girls.

"It'll be that perv who's been attacking women in the Domain!" said somebody.

"We'd better call the police!" said someone else.

"Let's grab him before he gets away," said one of the blokes. "There's enough of us here to hold him till the cops get here."

"They're my nieces!" I shouted at them. "Can't you hear them in there?"

"Filthy swine!" said the first woman, who obviously didn't want me to turn out to be anything but a depraved sex-maniac.

Now that was a bastard of a situation if ever there was one. A *real* bastard of a situation. And it didn't improve, either.

"Don't be so bloody stupid," I yelled at them. "They're only little girls."

And I held my hand up to show everyone how big they were.

"Oooo — listen to him!" said one of the women.

"Go and have a look," I said. "They're probably stuck in there. I don't think they can get the door open."

107

"Well they're not going to come out while *you're* here, are they mate?" said one of the blokes.

"Go and see for yourself," I said impatiently.

"No, thank you," he replied sarcastically. "It's not my cup of tea, that sort of thing."

"Not you, you bloody idiot," I said to him. And I turned to one of the women who hadn't been saying much and said to her, "Will *you* go in and get them. They'll be getting scared by this time."

"I'm not surprised," she said, backing away from me through the crowd as though I'd just indecently exposed myself. "You can hardly blame them, can you."

And in the bit of a lull that happened while they were waiting for me to think up an answer to that one, someone said, " There *is* somebody in there. Listen!"

And sure enough you could hear the kids, both of them, crying and yelling to be let out. But the mob made me get away from the door, in fact *all* the men did (and some of them got ready to grab me in case I made a run for it), while half a dozen women crowded into the women's toilet to investigate.

They brought the girls out and, no matter how hard they tried to get them to admit I'd been molesting them, they insisted that I was their uncle and we'd come to use the toilet. But although they had to let us go I was pretty sure most of them were disappointed that they hadn't apprehended a sexual pervert after all.

"Poor little things," I heard one of them say as we got back into the car.

Which goes to demonstrate that being the victim of an hysterical mob of outraged people is a bastard of a situation to be in.

21

Temperamental Bastard

I'VE PERSONALLY RUN INTO quite a few Temperamental Bastards (*Bastardus highstrungus*) in my time, but the man who stands out as the obvious one to use as an example is a bloke called Basil Wainwright, who I lived with for a few months once.

Basil wouldn't like to know I'd referred to him as a Temperamental Bastard. He used to claim he was a Sensitive Bastard (*Bastardus thinskinnus*), but I'm sticking to Temperamental B. because I refuse to let personal preferences sway me from my determination to be strictly factual in these matters of Bastardry.

Temperamental Bastards are not like us. We only see them as people who have to be very carefully approached until we've established what particular mood they're in this time. But the fact is that Unfeeling Bastards (*Bastardus icebergus*) like you and I just don't know what makes the Temperamental Bastard tick. He's away over our heads when it comes to appreciating the finer things in life.

He *feels* things we don't feel. He thinks things we just don't know about. He's usually engrossed either in exploring the psychological origins of his own suffering, or examining the deeper meanings of his relationships with other people. And he's so persistent in his claims of being absolutely honest that I'm downright bloody suspicious.

I must say that Basil was very patient and understanding with my inability to be patient an: understanding with him. In spite of his earnest lectures I'd still go gallivanting off with my current girlfriend to parties, dances, sailing, fishing, surfing and skiing — frivolous things like that. While Basil and his girl would sit around the flat having serious discussions about the deeper facets of their relationship.

This didn't seem to do much *for* their relationship, though, because they were always either just celebrating a reunion (with

Bastardus highstrungus

another serious discussion!), or parted — this time for ever — because of some unforgivable insensitivity on her part. Never his.

It was never quite clear to me exactly what these serious discussions were about. Sometimes they'd invite me to join in, and they'd get to talking about their mothers and fathers and uncles and aunts and cousins and brothers and sisters and friends and acquaintances, with such intense, analytical attention to detail that I'd eventually have to go to bed before I fell asleep where I was sitting. And sometimes I'd be woken up in the early hours of the morning by a fair-dinkum barney, as shrill and uninhibited as their serious discussion had been subdued and unemotional. Something had gone haywire somewhere along the way.

Although I used to go through a fair few girlfriends, Basil wasn't above changing his from time to time.

"Jenny and I have decided not to see each other for a while," he'd say. And you'd never see her again. Or, "Nola doesn't satisfy the *intellectual* side of my life," he'd say. And that would be the last we'd see of Nola. Or sometimes it'd be, "Penny doesn't understand my sensitivity," and Penny'd be a goner too.

For a Sensitive Bastard Basil could be pretty tough on his girlfriends when he'd had enough of them. That's why I prefer to describe him as a Temperamental Bastard.

As with most of the Temperamental Bastards you find huddled anxiously together in the cities, Basil was very careful not to get himself involved in anything to do with hard work. It was as though he was using up so much of his energy hanging onto his feelings that if he used any of it on anything else his sensitivity would start leaking out all over the place. He wasn't what you'd call a fit bloke, by any standards. He got very little sleep or exercise, he ate the most dreadful artificial tucker, and assaulted himself almost continuously with pills and capsules and all kinds of other medicinal drugs. He'd been doing all this to himself for years, and yet he was basically still quite healthy! It's truly astonishing the amount of punishment the human body can take.

I once dragged Basil off on a tramping holiday and nursed him along for five days, listening to his complaints about the primitive conditions, the food, the weather, his blisters and the general discomfort of it all. Then when we got back to town he spent

111

another week or so telling everyone how much good it had done him; how great he was feeling.

But then I suggested that he join a tramping club and make himself feel good every weekend and Basil dropped the whole subject. It was impossible, he said. Perhaps it was, but the reason he gave was that his creative work had to take precedence over everything else. I'd offended his sensitivity again by suggesting that a bit of exercise was more important than the pictures he painted whenever he was inspired. His paintings, incidentally, were as unfathomable as his way of living.

I don't know about you, tolerant reader — humanitarian Bastard (*Bastardus bigheartedus*) — but by the time I shifted out of that flat with Basil I'd just about enough of Temperamental Bastards. For too long we've been making excuses for them on the grounds of their sensitivity, as though to be sensitive was some kind of virtue.

Look at it this way, if you or I had a sensitive — say — elbow, we wouldn't be likely to regard it as anything but a disability, a source of discomfort. We certainly wouldn't claim it was a gift or a talent or an excuse to suffer, as the Temperamental Bastard so often does. We'd know that the best thing would be a rapid cure; a de-sentization of the elbow!

It's obvious enough that the T.B. is up against it in some way, even if we can't understand what his trouble is, but don't you think it's about time we gave up letting him prescribe his own treatment? I mean, if it was ever going to work it would have surely started to by this time! But it's not, it's getting worse. We've been listening to their jaundiced interpretation of their condition for so long now that we've forgotten what words like sensitive and temperamental really mean. The same kind of fact-dodgers have been slinging the word Creative around until we've lost track of the fact that it's meaningless. Man might be able to do a bit of re-arranging on a not-very-useful scale, but he can't create a single bloody thing — unless you can count situations, and most of the ones we've come up with so far are nothing to skite about.

112

22
Unlucky Bastard

STEVE CLAUSE WAS SUCH an Unlucky Bastard (*Bastardus rawdealus*) that it was hardly safe for him to get out of bed in the morning. I've never seen anything like it, fair go. It was uncanny. He had everything unlucky going for him that you could imagine, and yet he was such a Decent Bastard you couldn't help liking him.

I was working at the railway workshops when Steve got a job there, and from the very start he was in trouble. When I first started hanging around with him I didn't believe such bad luck could possibly last much longer, but I was wrong. If anything fell it'd be Steve it would land on. He could do things everyone else had been getting away with for years, and Steve'd get caught. Not that he was careless, just unlucky.

He'd been sacked from literally hundreds of jobs through sheer bad luck. I've never seen anything like it. As sure as he'd sneak away for a smoke the boss'd catch him at it.

He even lost his fiancee through bad luck. He was on his way to visit her one evening and stopped to grab a handful of flowers for her from the council gardens on his way through the park; and when he looked up there was a cop standing right there. Poor old Steve got the blame for every flower that had ever been pinched from the park. They decided to make an example of him. They fined him $15.00 and costs, and his fiancee's folks wouldn't let her have anything more to do with him because he had a criminal record.

And then he got the sack. Through bad luck. The blokes had been getting away with a staggering amount of perks from the job, but the night Steve decided to help himself to a handful of two-inch nails was the night they'd decided to spot-check the men at the gates. Steve was the only one they caught, and he was down the road again.

Just as I was getting on the bus with Steve that night outside

113

Bastardus rawdealus

work, one of the blokes called out that we'd better let the driver know he had Steve on board. I thought he was joking, but at the very first intersection we came to the bus collided with a truck, and Steve was the only passenger who got injured. He broke one of his front teeth on the handrail behind the seat in front of us and we couldn't find a dentist to put a cap on the exposed nerve in his broken tooth until the next day.

Steve had decided to take the ferry to the South Island to look for work down there so I took the day off and went to see him off. We shook hands on the wharf and he was walking innocently up the gangplank with everything he owned in a suitcase, when a scuffle started among some celebrating blokes who had come to see some of their mates off. One of them thought Steve was in on it and gave him a shove. And the shove, combined with Steve's bad luck, sent him somehow sailing down into the water between the boat and wharf, suitcase and all.

We finally twigged that Steve couldn't swim and an heroic onlooker dived in and held him up till they fished them out of the water, but they didn't bother with his suitcase.

They'd collared the bloke who'd pushed him and invited Steve to bring charges against him. But Steve refused. He maintained that he would probably have fallen into the harbour anyway and the wharf police had to let the bloke go in the finish. It was obvious that the police thought he was some kind of nut, but I didn't. I'd known Steve for a couple of months by this time and wasn't a bit surprised that him trying on something like getting onto a big ferryboat had ended in disaster.

He'd lost his ferry ticket along with everything else and they wouldn't believe he'd ever had a ticket in the first place, so he couldn't go on the ferry. He was still wringing wet from his dip in the harbour and it was as cold as hell, so I decided to take him back to my flat and get him into some dry clothes.

I should have known better. The landlady sprung me sneaking this wet bedraggled Steve into my flat and she kept us bailed up on the stairs to remind me of her rules about drinking and parties and visitors and other such immoral carryings-on in the flat. We were just getting away from her when she spotted Steve's puddle of water on her carpet and did her block good and proper.

115

She didn't look like stopping for a while so I dragged Steve inside and shut the door, which she knocked on a little later to give me a week's notice to get out of the place.

We dried Steve's clothes in front of the heater and that night he slept on my couch. In the morning I gave him some of my clothes and stuff and we packed it into an old kit I had. I had just over sixty dollars and lent Steve thirty dollars of it to tide him over. I decided to take the day off work and personally deliver him to the ferry, but before we'd got to the wharf some blokes with a movie camera set up on the footpath stopped us. I wanted us to cut and run for it before any bad luck happened, but before I could get Steve to take off they'd collared him to tell television-land what he thought about the Common Market developments.

He mumbled something non-committal into their microphone and I was dragging him away before something happened when it did. Someone in the small crowd that had gathered suddenly shouted, "Hey, There's Steve Clause!" And I could tell by the way they said it that here was more bad luck. I was right. A great big bloke and his even bigger mate skinned us for forty dollars Steve had borrowed off him once and forgotten to pay back.

And when we looked around for Steve's kit of gear it was gone. Somebody had pinched it and nobody had seen them do it. So he had no gear or money again.

By the time I'd bought Steve's ticket on the ferry and given him a ten-dollar stake to help him get a job down south I had exactly 75 cents left out of my sixty dollars. My resources were exhausted. There was nothing more I could do for him.

My feelings as the boat pulled away from the wharf were not mixed. I shouted to Steve to stand farther back from the rail and hoped nothing would happen to stop that ferry. I'd done all that could be humanly expected of me. It was somebody else's turn now.

I just managed to hang onto my job for taking two days off without telling them, and I got a much better flat to live in. It was three months before I heard from Steve. Only a letter, but even that made me slightly apprehensive. He sent three dollars and a little note saying he'd hoped to send more but he'd been a bit unlucky. I had no option but to believe him.

23
Vain Bastard

H E CARRIES A COMB and always has a clean handkerchief in his pocket. And that, good reader, is as much as I know about the Vain Bastard (*Bastardus primpus*). I hadn't realised until I undertook to write about him that I'd never had much to do with them. I can't think of a single really Vain Bastard I've known personally.

This must be put right at once, a little research is called for. Wait here — I'm going down town to find a Vain Bastard and get to know him. I'll let you know how I get on when I get back.

LATER — You may not realise this, patient reader, but sixteen hours have passed since you finished reading the above paragraph. I've been down town and looked through some of the pubs for a Vain Bastard. It didn't take as long as I'd expected. I found a beaut in the lounge bar of the Brit. Immaculate, he was, standing there at the bar. Fussy, finnicky and fastidious. Creases in all the right places. In short — resplendent.

It was only when I approached him to introduce myself that I realised I'd been so engrossed in the hunt for a Vain Bastard I hadn't given any thought to what I was going to do when I'd caught one. I decided to play it by ear.

As I reached my quarry I saw why it was that I'd never got close to any Vain Bastards before. There's something about me that makes them distinctly uneasy. This one shrank away from me as though I might at any moment spatter all over his beautiful clothes. But he relaxed a little as he realised that unless I actually touched him none of my scruffiness was going to rub off on his resplendency.

"G'day," I said, "How's it going?"

"Quite well, thank you," he said cautiously.

"Nice day for it," I observed, signalling for the barman to fill my new friend's glass and bring me one of the same.

Bastardus primpus

"Yes it is," he replied fastidiously.

"I'm Barry Crump," I said, holding out my hand for him to shake.

He looked at my hand as though it was dripping with waste-oil, and then when it didn't go away again he shook it.

"Philip —," he said. "Have we met before?"

"Don't think so," I said. "What are you doing for a crust these days?"

"I'm not working at the moment," he said, as though I should have known.

"Waiting for someone?" I asked him.

"Yes, I am, as a matter of fact," he replied. "— Mother," he added, as though it might frighten me off. "We're going to lunch as soon as she gets here."

"Good idea," I nodded. "You've got to eat. I might even join you. Where do you eat usually?"

Well his mother didn't turn up and I eventually dragged my captive Vain Bastard off for a feed at a flash restaurant. Shouted us two bottles of imported plonk to see if there was any vitality under all his plumage, but nothing happened so I carted him off to another pub for a few more snorts. But when I picked up a couple of girls for us to have a night out on the town with, Philip vanished in the direction of the toilet and we didn't see him again. So I had to manage the girls on my own. The whole thing turned out a bit expensive, but I had the information I needed for this discourse on Vain Bastards.

And this, going on what I gleaned from my day with the timid Philip, is what I learned about them.

The Vain Bastard is a hard man to get to know because he's so heavily disguised. It's hard to tell what he's like by the look of him because he's camouflaged by his fancy-dress costume and his hair is so strictly regimented into the shape and style he thinks he looks best in.

And because he's such a Vain Bastard you can't tell what he's like from what he says because he's only interested in subjects pertaining to himself, providing they're flattering subjects. They don't like talking about anything that's not clean and sweet-smelling, and it's no good trying to talk to them at all while you're

119

walking along a city street with them because they're too pre-occupied with catching their reflection in shop windows to keep a conversation going.

You can't tell what he's like by his movements because they're influenced so much by the care he thinks he needs to take not to crease or soil his clothes. He walks stiff-legged so as not to put knees in his trousers, and when he sits he perches on his chair as though expecting it to splinter under his weight and deposit him on the dusty carpet any moment.

He eats as though each forkful of food might explode all over his shirt-front before he can get it safely into his mouth, and he's as fussy about his health as he is about his appearance. He's got a thing about germs and believes that to get wet means to get pneumonia.

He uses the toilet, combs his hair, and then washes his hands. He's a fan for jewellery and a sucker for the con-men who manufacture cosmetics. He smells like a whore's handbag of some kind of scent they've put a masculine-sounding label on and conned him into buying by suggesting on television that no woman worth her salt would have anything to do with him unless he reeks of the stuff.

He's dishonest and unreliable because his immediate require-ments are much more important than any arrangement he may have previously condescended to make with a member of the common herd. And there's nothing he couldn't do better than the experts if only he bothered to put a little time and practice into it. Poor Vain Bastard.

24
Weak Bastard

NONE OF US DISPUTED that Cedric Fleet was a Weak Bastard (*Bastardus dishwaterus*) from the time he first turned up asking for a job on the Rabbit Board. But none of us realised just how weak he really was. You could see he was weak just by looking at him. There was nothing of him, for a start. Scrawny, wizened, middle-aged and wretched-looking. I put his weight at around six-and-a-half to seven stone. He was almost five foot high when he stood up straight, which wasn't often. He went round hunched over a like a sick man.

"Do you think you could stand up to the work?" the boss asked, looking him up and down.

"I don't know," he said. "I've been a bit crook on it lately."

"Well we need men, I'll give you a trial," said the boss. "You can share the end hut with Crumpy here. He'll show you where to put your gear."

So Cedric moved in with me. The boss told me on the quiet to keep an eye on him, but there was hardly enough of him to keep a decent eye on. I gave him a hand to lift his three big suitcases of gear up the steps into the hut and as soon as we'd got his bunk made up he hoisted his miserable frame into it and flaked out. That didn't matter because new blokes always got a day on full pay to settle in. He didn't even want to eat when I woke up for a feed that night, so I ate it myself and left him asleep.

The next day was Saturday and some of us were going into town to the pub, so I woke Cedric up to see if he wanted to come. But he only drank a cup of tea or two and told me he'd better stay home because the last time he'd gone on the bash he'd ended up with a dose of double-pneumonia.

I stayed in town that night and when I got back to camp next day Cedric was sitting on the edge of his bunk looking anxiously into his shaving mirror.

Bastardus dishwaterus

"I think I'm coming down with something," he said to me. "My tongue's a funny colour."

"So's mine," I told him. "Let's get this hut cleaned up and put a feed on."

That's when I discovered that Cedric couldn't stay in the hut while the floor was being swept because it might bring on his hay-fever. And a bit later I discovered that he had to be very careful what he ate. Most things, it seemed, disagreed with him.

"I've got to watch my health, you know," he said.

"What health?" I couldn't help asking.

I thought I was going to carry him out to the truck when they came to pick us up the next morning, but he made it all right. Then he told the boss he had a rare disease called haemophilia and had to ride in the front of the truck in case he cut himself and bled to death. We didn't know whether to believe him or not but we weren't game to take the risk, so Cedric always rode in the front, just in case.

We were laying poison at the time and every day we'd give Cedric a half-full jam-gun and let him do the easy spots around the truck until he got a bit of his health back. But he never did. He got weaker, if anything, and almost every day he informed us of some new and frightful disability he suffered from.

He'd had one lung removed, and one kidney. He'd had operations on his appendix, his gall-bladder, his back and his ulcers. He was allergic to seventy-eight of the ninety things you *could* be allergic to. He had a steel pin in his ankle and a plate in his hip. (His bones were powdery and brittle because of some deficiency or other). He sure knew a lot of long medical words, and when you looked at him, no matter what outrageous-sounding disease he claimed to be suffering from this time, you simply had to give him the benefit of the doubt.

Weak Bastards usually have a ton of guts to make up for their lack of strength, but not our Cedric. He was weak in all departments. He had neither strength *nor* guts. He complained so long and so convincingly about his ebbing vitality that he was never sent down into gullies for fear he wouldn't make it back up to the top again. We'd hurry to lift things for him or help him over

123

fences or logs. He never had to get out of the truck and open gates, or chop firewood, or do any cooking. He was just too weak.

Although none of us actually said so at the time, we all had a sneaking concern that we might have to carry him back to camp feet-first one of these days, in spite of all we could do to conserve his feeble reserves of energy.

The boss had our sympathy. Even if Cedric had pulled his own weight it wouldn't have been noticeable, and he couldn't even do *that* half the time, let alone a day's work. But you couldn't sack a man out of his job when he was in the condition Cedric was in. So we went on nursing him along and reassuring ourselves that he might start coming right any day now, though none of us really believed it was possible.

And then one morning, just as we were climbing into the truck, one of the blokes yelled out, "Hey . . . what's all that smoke! It looks as though your hut's on fire!"

And it surely did. There was smoke pouring out of the doorway.

"Get some water!" shouted the boss. And we ran to get buckets and things to fight the fire with. But none of us was as quick as Cedric.

"My things are in there!" he shouted. And he ran like a hare to the hut and dived straight into the smoke. And the next thing we knew there was a veritable shower of things flying out through the door. First all his personal gear — clothes and books and things — then all my stuff. Then the pots and billies and all the food out of the cupboards. Chairs, bedding, tools, lamps, cases, boxes, sacks, benches and bags. There was a lot of gear in that hut, some of it weighing more than Cedric, and every bit of it came flying out through that door as though there were two strong men behind it.

Cedric was so engrossed in clearing out the hut that he hadn't noticed the smoke clearing. There were only a few whiffs of it still drifting around by the time he ran out dragging the big sheepskin mat off the floor. When he saw us all standing there he stopped and looked back into the conflagration, but there was none.

To say that he looked as sheepish as the mat he was holding, as he stood there amongst all the stuff he'd thrown out of the hut, would be an understatement.

124

"I thought I'd make sure nothing got burnt," he said.

We had a look and found that a pair of Cedric's trousers had fallen off the drying-rail into the embers of the fire. They'd smouldered away to a charred black mess. Apart from that the only damage was the stuff that got broken when Cedric slung it out of the hut with such astonishing strength and energy.

The little bastard was as tough as machine-belting. He'd been using his scrawny appearance to take us for a ride. And we had to admit he'd done it handsomely. He'd been having a holiday at our expense. Needless to say he didn't get any change out of us after that, but we didn't get any work out of him either. As soon as he saw that his jig was up he packed it in.

"I'll have to go back up north before the winter sets in," he told the boss. "I have to watch me rheumatics, y'know."

And the boss paid him off without comment.

25
Xenial Bastard

THE ONLY THING I know about this kind of Bastard —
Xenial Bastard (*Bastardus obscurus*) — is that somebody
called me one once. And I've returned the schoolmistress's
dictionary so I don't know whether I was being praised, criticised,
or taken the micky out of.

I'd like to believe she said *Genial* Bastard, but I know she didn't.
Anyway, I've never met a Bastard yet who had an accurate idea
of his own B-rating, and I don't suppose I'm any different from
any other Bastard.

The surest way of finding out would be to ask someone who
knows me, and he'll tell you, instantly and accurately, precisely
what sort of Bastard I am; but ask him what sort of Bastard he
himself is and he'll become evasive, inarticulate and often either
falsely modest or boastful or totally dishonest. Whatever he says,
the chances of him being able to give himself an accurate B-rating
are millions to one — that is, according to a survey I've been
carrying out since 1935.

Which just goes to show that if we knew as much about
ourselves as we claim to know about other people there'd be more
Splendid Bastards like you and me around.

Bastardus obscurus

Bastardus obscurus

Ferron

26
Young Bastard

YOUNG BASTARDS (*BASTARDUS WHIPPER-SNAPPERUS*) are
known to everybody all over the world. The main thing
about Youngbastardry is that it's seldom permanent and
most of the types of Bastard described in this priceless collection
were themselves Young Bastards in their time.

The Young Bastard swipes your fruit, rides his bike into your
hedge or flower garden, throws stones onto your lawn, breaks
the odd window with his slug-gun or shanghai, asks endless
questions and generally exasperates us cantankerous Old Bastards
(*Bastardus senilus*). He might shout a bit of cheek when you
drive past if he's with a couple of other Young Bastards. He
may even whip the money out of your milk bottles if you don't
watch it.

If you know a Young Bastard well, you can often pick what
kind of Bastard he's going to grow up into, but apart from guiding
him as well as you can away from the more odious types of
Bastardry there's nothing much you can do about it, because by
this time his Bastard-type is well and truly settled.

The Young Bastard has an aversion to Old Bastards like you
and me trying out our various psychological theories on how to
"handle" Young Bastards like him. He finds it very difficult to
take anyone seriously who doesn't remember what it was like to
be a Young Bastard.

So the next time a Young Bastard gets on your goat, ask
yourself how many goats you got on when you were a Young
Bastard yourself. Then give him a grin, tell him he's a Young
Bastard, and he's your friend for life. You're talking his language.

You may have noticed just back there where I said that Youngbastardry is *seldom* permanent. That was to allow for the alarm-
ing numbers of us (not you or I, of course) who never grow up.
People who retain intact all the tantrums, the complaining-to-
their-mothers, the demands and the freedom from responsibility

Bastardus whipper-snapperus

of their childhood, and yet they still insist on having all the privileges that go with adulthood.

They want the best of everything they've ever had, *when* they want it. And they also want to *not* have it when it's inconvenient. This type of Youngbastardry is mostly found in so-called men, but not exclusively (E.g. the fat woman with the voice and the uncontrolled appetites of an infant.) And the places you find these specimens! The headmaster complaining to his assembled pupilage that he can't go on putting up with some piece of adolescent behaviour or other. ("It's not fair!")

The politician — whining to the nation on television about the dreadfulness of the opposition or the trade unions. ("You kids are going to get us all into trouble!")

The magistrate who tells the peeping-Tom how he has to have beasts like him locked up for the protection of decent people. ("You're not allowed over to our place to play any more, so ha!")

And the unheroic credit manager of a department store who's done a quick check-up on you through his shabby system and tells you he's afraid he is unable to offer you a credit account at the moment. ("Your granny's got something bad wrong with her, so ha!")

The more you think of it the more of them there are. It's a sobering thing to contemplate. If you ask me the less these types have to do with bringing up, or even influencing, our genuine Young Bastards the better.

I was even starting to suspect myself for a moment there.

27

Zealous Bastard

I T DISTRESSES ME TO have to end this section with the description of the Zealous Bastard (*Bastardus fanaticus*), but this is no time to depart from the strict observance of outspoken, unperjured veracity that sets this volume apart from its imitators. So here goes.

The Zealous Bastard, mercifully, seldom appears amongst us, but when he does there's not much doubt about it. The only snag about recognising him is that it's sometimes difficult not to mistake him for the Humanitarian Bastard (*Bastardus philanthropus*), and *that* would be a mistake.

Of all the Bastards from the Onward and Upward Department the Zealous Bastard takes the cake as far as enthusiasm goes, and Ira Bowmast was a fair-dinkum beaut. You could tell that by the look of him. He looked like a cartoon of a religious racing car. He was a high-octane glass of milk, or a Pomeranian pig-dog. He was clear-eyed and hairy, skinny and overpowering, meek and intimidating. He used to get around in a balaclava, three big jumpers (summer and winter), and enormous overcoat, and Roman sandals with dirty toenails.

He'd appear amongst us and really take up the cudgels on behalf of somebody (never himself) or something, usually some cause or other. But it was always something that wasn't topical, something out of date and unpopular. Something everyone else had lost or never had any interest in. The last time it was getting the Yanks out of Vietnam and most of them were already gone, but Ira accumulated more support for that cause than it had ever had when it was at the height of its fashion.

He'd pursue his chosen objective with a truly inspiring vigour. He'd work so energetically, so purposefully, and with such fervent and consuming, single-minded tenacity that we could only stand back and admire him and leave him to it.

By his very self-denial he usually engendered a fair number of

Bastardus fanaticus

setbacks, but these only seemed to spur him on to even greater efforts, until, one by one, his obstacles were overwhelmed by his sheer unfaltering drive and dedication. And at last his goal would be in sight. The result was a foregone conclusion. The bureaucrats were willing to negotiate with him. Employers were prepared to discuss changes in the working conditions of their downtrodden employees or the government was announcing a preliminary investigation into the possible setting-up of another Royal Commission. . . .

And then, to everyone's astonishment, with the victory he'd worked so long and ardently for within his very grasp, the bastard would go and lose interest in it. As often as not he'd just disappear, leaving all his supporters wondering what the hell to do now.

Every time this happened we'd swear never to take any notice of him ever again, but he'd turn up after two, or six, or twelve months and before we'd know what was happening he'd have us handing out leaflets, or drumming up support for his new cause in some other way. It was hard not to believe that this time it was the real thing. Ira would be so bloody convincing; striving and battling valiantly onward, against all odds and opposition.

Then, just when it looked as though we were really getting somewhere, he'd announce that he was needed up north to help with the Treaty of Waitangi cause, or some such. We'd been had again.

And there's not much you can do about it when you've been caught up in the whirl of enthusiasm that surrounds a Zealous Bastard. He's not humanitarian — as you thought, nor is he ambitious, nor is he particularly interested in what he's been fighting *for*. It's the long, gruelling, up-hill struggle he's interested in — the might-and-main of it all. The challenge of the thing. And there's no challenge in being victorious. Winning a battle simply means to the Zealous Bastard that he has to turn round and find something else to get stuck into. It's the end of the game for him, he's been bowled out . . .

I hadn't thought of it that way before. Wait till I see that **Zealous Bastard Ira Bowmast again!**

134

HERE ARE A FEW OTHER BASTARDS I MET AFTER COMPLETING MY A-Z OF BASTARDRY

Introduction

WELL IT HAS BEEN a year or three since I produced my alphabetical list of bastards, and since then I have spent the best part of twelve months down on the Coast — at a place called Tangaroa which I disliked from the start but had quite a job escaping from. It was one of those small, damp and scattered places — in some respects thirty years out of date, and fifty years in others, but it boasted as concentrated a collection of bastards you could ever hope to meet in this fair land.

My triumphal entry into Tangaroa was heralded only by a shower of rain and an old brown dog that was lying in the middle of the road outside the store. The town was: a deceptively innocent-looking old pub; a hall that was never used; about a dozen huts and houses; a store/post office with two petrol bowsers; and, just down the road, a long bridge over the Tangaroa River.

I stopped at the petrol pumps and went in to the store. The place was open but there was no-one around. I waited for a while and then rapped on the counter with a fifty-cent coin. But no-one came.

"Shop!" I called out.

Nothing.

"Anyone there?" I yelled.

No-one.

So I went outside. The back door of the house beside the store was open so I went over and knocked.

No response.

I drove along to the pub and went in. There was no-one there. I rapped on the bar with a coin and after a while I heard footsteps so I stopped rapping. But the footsteps hadn't heard me at all. They faded away to a different part of the building.

"Whew!" I said to myself to the mirror behind the bar. I wasn't in any particular hurry but this was bloody ridiculous. Just then

137

someone pulled up outside the pub in one of those Volkswagen buggies towing a trailer loaded with gear, with a little plywood dinghy tied on the top. It looked like some kind of camping outfit but it was impossible to tell what the bloke did by looking at him or his gear. He seemed to have a hell of a lot of sacks and netting and there was a big bundle of flax tied on to the load. He had come a long way by the look of it. The whole outfit, including himself, was splattered with mud.

He got out of his waggon and came into the bar. A big rough-looking bloke with two fingers missing off his left hand and a face like a fritter. He had red hair starting to go grey and was wearing anything you like. He also needed a shave but if you were going to clean him up it would be a fair while before you got around to that.

"G'day," he said.

"G'day," I nodded back.

"What do you do to get a drink around here?" asked the bloke.

"You wait," I said.

So we waited. The big bloke was Nobby Corcoran, who had come over from Canterbury to have a crack at eeling in some of the lakes on the Coast. He had already jacked up to sell his eels to the bloke who ran a venison freezer, four miles down the road, for eight cents a pound, which he reckoned wasn't a bad price.

It wasn't long before the publican turned up. He was Rex Logan — dark, fattish, born and bred on the Coast, proud of it and in no hurry. He had a big wife who looked and talked and dressed and walked just like Rex, except that she did most of the work around the pub and Rex did most of the talking.

Rex had to muck around with his beer system for a while before we got a drink but when we finally did the first few beers were on the house. The more beer we knocked back, the better Nobby and I hit it off. Nobby could use an off-sider and I had nothing to do and nowhere that I had to get to, so we decided to have a go at eeling Lake Douglas together and see how it worked out.

Nobby was a Simple Bastard (*Bastardus straightforwardus*) — not just an honest bastard (*Bastardus truthus*) like you or I, but in spite of being a bit rough at the edges, generous and kind.

138

Nobby and I spent all next day getting gas and supplies from the store and in the afternoon we moved in to a disused Forest Service hut down the road from Tangaroa and nine miles from Lake Douglas. It seemed that I was going to stay in the locality for a while, although I'm not at all sure I would have done what I did if I had realised just what an assortment of bastards I'd meet in Tangaroa. They were too good to miss, so here goes.

Billy

29
Simple Bastard

IN SPITE OF HIM being a bit on the rough side, I could tell that Nobby was going to be a good bloke to camp and work with. It'd probably take plenty to get him worried or rattled, and probably a hell of a lot more to quieten him down again once he got his rag out. When he had something to say, he said it. And when he said something it was exactly what he meant, neither more or less. And when he didn't have anything to say, he didn't say anything.

He didn't even know how to be sarcastic.

It rained for four days and we spent most of the time in the pub. Our money was just about cut by the time we arrived at the lake with Nobby's boat and his seven chicken-netting eel-traps on the back of my ute.

Lake Douglas was dark and deep and still and clear, with trees and moss right down to the water, except for three or four small beaches of sand and reeds. The vegetation was so thick the lake reminded me of the tropics, but that was as far as any similarity went. This one was so cold it hurt.

We baited the traps with dead hares we'd picked up on the road and it took us several hours to get them spaced out across the lake because the boat would only take two of us and two of the traps at once. Nobby rowed his boat like he did everything else — bloody clumsily. One oar was longer than the other; rowlocks kept slipping out of their holes; there was only three inches of freeboard, and I had to balance the boat and bail out water. She leaked.

"Do you reckon it's safe to wear those gumboots of yours in the boat, Nobby?" I asked.

"Why not?" said Nobby, splashing me with a freezing oarful of water.

"Well, if we were to capsize you wouldn't be able to swim too good with them on."

Bastardus straightforwardus

"I can't swim at all with them on or off," grinned Nobby, "so it doesn't make any difference. This'll do, we'll drop one about here."

I eased one of the baited traps over the stern. It was six or seven feet long and I had to be careful not to tip the boat over too far. I let the trap down on its rope, but before it was completely out of sight, came to the half-gallon plastic detergent container Nobby used for a float.

"The rope's too short," I said. "The hinaki's nowhere near the bottom yet."

"Blast," said Nobby. "Never thought of that. the place I've been working in is only shallow. Hang on to it, I'll tow us into shallow water."

Which took nearly half an hour. We extended the ropes on our traps with whatever we could find in the way of rope, and wire, and flax, and it was well into the afternoon by the time we'd finished laying them. Then we drove into Tangaroa and spent an hour and a half looking for and waiting for the bloke at the store so we could buy some rope and bread off him. We couldn't afford to wait in the pub any more. We had less than a dollar left by the time we paid for the stuff we bought.

"Doesn't matter," said Nobby. "We'll be selling eels tomorrow."

"I just hope we catch some," I said.

Nobby grinned at me. "If we don't, I'll give you my share of the catch," he said.

But it'd take more than that to reassure a bloke who'd never given eels a second thought in his life.

It rained all night and it was still raining next morning when we got up early. We got the fire going, had tea and toast, coats on, and away to the lake to see what we'd got. The rain stopped as we arrived. We tipped the rainwater out of the dinghy and Nobby rowed us out to the farthest trap-float. On the way there I idly wondered how on earth Nobby could have had so much experience at rowing a boat and still be so downright bad at it.

It was at the first trap we lifted that I found out why Nobby had use for a mate. I thought the trap must have been snagged on something at first, but it was full of eels — packed with them.

142

About seventy or eighty pounds weight and some bloody whoppers amongst them! They were even spilling out through the neck of the trap as I managed to roll it over the stern into the boat. Nobby had to sit right up in the front to keep the stern from going under. Then Nobby leaned forward and held a sack open while I released the gate at the end of the trap and the whole load slid neatly into the sack. Nobby tied the neck of the nearly-full sack with flax while I baited the trap again and lowered it back over the stern.

"How the hell do you pull 'em up on your own without capsizing the boat?" I asked, shoving a stray slithering eel into a fresh sack with my foot.

"Rocks," said Nobby.

"Rocks?"

"Yeah. You load the back of the boat up with as many rocks as she'll take and row out to your hinaki. Then you shift the rocks into the front of the boat so you can get into the back of it and pull the hinaki in. When you've got enough eels you just chuck the rocks over the side and use the sacks of eels to balance the boat. It's a hell of a lot easier with two blokes, though, isn't it?" he added.

"I can believe that," I said with feeling. "But why not get a bigger boat?"

"It'd be too tough to cart around and handle," said Nobby. "Some of the places I get into are pretty swampy and shallow. This boat'll do us. You should see some of the tidal estuaries over the other side. This is nothing."

"It's something all right," I said. "But I think I can imagine what you mean."

The other six traps were all as full as the first one and it was about three hours before we had our seven nearly-full sacks of all sized yellow-bellies on the back of the ute. I could tell we had a fair load by the way the ute handled.

"Would you call this good going?" I asked Nobby.

"Not particularly," said Nobby. "You always do pretty good at first. We could clean 'em out of that lake in a week or so. We'll just have to wait and see how it goes."

The bloke at the venison freezer, a Dutchman, weighed our

sacks of eels and then emptied them into one of four 500-gallon concrete water tanks he had, fresh water running through from a spring up in the bush behind his place.

"What happens to them now?" I wanted to know.

"I keep 'em alive in the tanks for two or three weeks," explained the eel bloke. "Then I kill 'em and smoke 'em. He waved his arm towards a longish building where all this killing and smoking evidently took place.

"What do you do with them then?"

"Export," said the bloke. "Most of my stuff goes to Holland."

Then he weighed the wet sacks and deducted that from the total he'd written on the back of his docket book.

"I make it 496 pounds," he said. "That okay?"

"Yep," said Nobby.

And at eight cents a pound the bloke wrote them out a cheque for $39.68.

Driving back to the hut I said, "That's not bad money, Nobby. I make it roughly 280 bucks a week. That's 140 each. These eels are really something!"

"Yeah," said Nobby, with a non-commital grin of someone who knows it never really works out that way.

If someone had told me I was going to get a kick out of catching eels in a freezing Westland lake and actually make money at it — I'd have simply felt sorry for them. But I did. The traps kept catching day after day and even Nobby seemed mildly surprised. The locals were beginning to thaw out a bit and some of them even waved or nodded when we drove past or walked into the pub.

In the mornings when the mist was lifting off the surface of the lake and the sun was flooding across the Alps, but not yet high enough to reach into the valleys, the water reflected the snowy craggy cloud-streaked peaks of the mountains and the bushed ridges leading up to them like a giant mirror. And the air was as clear and chill as the water in the lake itself. I couldn't remember seeing anything better-looking.

For a man who'd been making his living for five years by taking eels out of lakes and rivers and estuaries by the ton, Nobby knew

144

astonishingly little about them. He knew they ate meat and were partial to the odd trout or two, but nothing else about their diet. He knew they were supposed to migrate and breed out in the sea somewhere, but he'd never seen it. He knew there was a difference between a silver-belly and a yellow-belly, but apart from the colour of them they were all the same to him. Eels — eight cents a pound. Nobby was a simple bastard.

And when the eels in their traps began to dwindle down to 150 to 200 pounds a day, I shot the odd deer or two up in the big Tangaroa River flats by getting out before daylight in the morning and stalking quietly along the misty bush-edges in the first light. We both laughed at the idea of Nobby sneaking quietly enough to get within rifle shot of a deer and shared the money we got for the meat.

Nobby was a tower of strength when it came to packing out the deer, which weighed up to 175 pounds a carcass. The locals seemed to think I was a pretty good sort of a hunter because they hardly ever shot any deer, and the two professional hunters with their jet-boat had hardly got any either. But then they seldom got out before daylight and went hunting for them. They didn't need to, it was their locality and the way they saw it every deer shot was shot by everyone.

I didn't bother telling anyone that the first deer I shot I had to carry back to the hut, head, guts and all, because I'd forgotten to take a knife with me.

It had to happen that our catch of eels fell off until it was uneconomic, but Lake Douglas kept us going for three weeks before Nobby made up his mind to lift his traps and head further south to try some of the lakes down there. But I had got to like the meat-hunting and the money that was in it so I decided to stick around Tangaroa for a while.

We loaded Nobby's waggon and trailer and then got so drunk having a send-off noggin or two in the pub that he couldn't leave till the next day. He set off in the middle of a mind-blowing hangover, waving his three-fingered hand out the window of his VW — and got his two off-side wheels off the track into a patch of swamp and reeds and I had to tow him out with the ute.

Let's face it, Simple Bastards like Nobby are not too bad to have around, and I rather missed my big clumsy mate, even if I was too busy to think about it much. I hunted morning and evening and had to go so far up the river to have a shot that my new-found mates at the Tangaroa pub could have been excused it they'd started calling me an Enthusiastic Bastard (*Bastardus keenus*). It was as though most of the deer had followed Nobby south, so I decided to stick around and have a go at this whitebaiting I'd been hearing so much about. I started making a few casual enquiries and discovered that although every Tangaroan knew everything there was to know about it . . .

30
Rough Bastard

SCRATCHER FARRELL WAS THE bloke to see about whitebaiting. He was one of the most successful whitebaiters on the Coast, they reckoned. Been at it more than twenty years and always got more than anyone else.

He liked working with a mate, but for some reason that wasn't quite clear no one ever stayed with him for more than a week or two. Everyone agreed that Scratcher had something wrong with him, but no one seemed to be able to say exactly what it was, except that he "lived a bit hard". I found out *where* he lived a bit hard, about five miles away down a dead-end side road and went to see him.

I got to know Scratcher pretty well over the next few weeks. He was a little wiry bloke about fifty or sixty years old. Sometimes you couldn't get a word out of him and sometimes you could, depending on how you struck him. He told me a bit about whitebaiting in one of his talkative moods and made out a list of the things I was going to need. It was written with a sharpened .22 bullet on a flap torn off a cardboard box.

Scratcher lived a bit hard all right — he was a Real Rough Bastard (*Bastardus hardcasus*). He lived in a draughty old shed with a dirt floor. He cooked his tucker in buckets over a smoky fire in the doorway. The stuff in plastic buckets only got as cooked as it could by having boiling water from one of his galvanised buckets poured into it. You had to literally duck through the flames and smoke to get inside when he had a feed on. When the wind was blowing the smoke into the shed he did his cooking and eating from the outside, and when it wasn't he could operate from inside, more or less out of the rain.

Everything in the shed was hanging from nails around the dry areas of the walls. The dirt floor soaked up the water from outside when it rained and it was often quite muddy. His bunk was the corrugated-iron door off the shed, built up from the floor

147

Bastardus hardcasus

with blocks of firewood and padded with sacks and coats and his good going-to-town clothes.

For light in the daytime we hung the sack over the one window opening on a nail to one side.

At night he used a candle shielded from the draught by a milk-powder tin cut down the middle. He didn't trust pressure lamps and he didn't like the smell of kerosene. He usually went to bed early anyway, he told me.

Most of his food hung from the roof in sacks with slits cut in them so he could put stuff in and get it out again without having to take his cupboards down. Anything perishable had to be kept in the cab of his old Land Rover because that was the only possum-and-waterproof place he had access to. Every three months or so he got them to send him down a sack of calf milk-powder, a fifty-pound bag of flour, and twenty large tins of golden syrup. The rest of his stuff he got from the store or picked up around the place. He wasn't fussy about what he ate and he used to shoot quite a few birds and hares and things to put in his buckets of stew. He was always on the scrounge for meat and they reckoned he'd pinch the maggotty rib-cage of a goat off one of Ted Packer's dogs, but they were probably exaggerating.

The one good thing about Scratcher and his food was that he didn't like giving any away. I dropped in to see him one morning and Scratcher was eating a skinned, but not gutted, shag he'd shot. He'd fried it in his shovel and was tearing into it with the blackened stumps of his few remaining teeth as though he'd seen me coming and didn't want to have to offer me any. We yarned while he finished his meal and wiped his face on his hands and then his hands on his pants. We then went on chatting about nothing in particular while Scratcher messed about in his open-air kitchen. I then suddenly noticed that he was squeezing something out of a tube into a bucketful of something he had been boiling over the fire.

"Hey, that's not *glue* you're putting in there, is it Scratcher?"

Scratcher had a look at the tube. "Yeah, looks like it," he said.

"You can't eat that stuff!"

"Why not?" said Scratcher, squeezing a bit more in and wiping the nozzle of the tube on the rim of the bucket.

"You'll make yourself crook."

"No, it's okay," said Scratcher. "I put some in the stew by accident the other night and it thickened her up just nicely. It was a bit dark at the time and I thought it was condensed milk," he explained.

"Is there *anything* you wouldn't eat?" I asked.

Scratcher thought this over for a few moments.

"Don't go much on dogs," he said "Or . . ."

"Do you ever go up to town, Scratcher?"

"Yeah, I was up there a few months back."

"Stay long?"

"No, I only wanted to see me sister's kids and buy a few things."

"Well, did you see them?"

"See who?"

"Your sister's kids."

"Oh, them. Yeah, I saw them there. They were playing around in the yard. Everything looked all right so I came away again."

"You mean to say you didn't even go in and have a yarn with them?"

"No, I didn't want to talk to 'em. I only wanted to see if they were okay."

"Well, did you get your shopping done?"

"No, everything was shut, so I came home. Must have been a Sunday or something."

"You mean you drove 250 miles and back just to look at your sister's kids?"

"Yeah, I don't like the towns much."

There was the day I went out to have a look at Scratcher's job with him. It was his official duty to maintain the telephone line between Tangaroa and Boulder Creek, a tiny settlement in the next valley. It was a single wire running through insulators hammered into the trees, roughly nine miles of it, most of it through heavy bush. Whenever a tree or branch fell across the wire they'd let Scratcher know the phone was out and he'd go and walk along the line until he found the break and fix it.

As soon as I saw the line I discovered why it was so notoriously weak. Scratcher had been tying the breaks in the wire with all

150

sorts of stuff. It was incredible that the line worked at all. Quite a few of the gaps were bridged with *barbed* wire, and in one place, where he hadn't been quite able to get the broken ends of wire to meet he'd punched holes in each end of a sardine tin and hooked the wires into them. He'd used a length of dog-chain in one place, and a hook made out of a rusty four-inch nail in another. In another spot he'd used an iron fencing-standard and in another a billy-handle; in another a slasher-head — a stirrup iron . . .

"Hey Scratcher, you can't do this!" I said, kicking at a push-bike wheel that hung nearly to the ground in an old break in the wire.

"Why not?" said Scratcher. "That's been there for months. I brought up a spring-leaf to replace it once, but I had to use it in another place. This works okay though."

"Don't they give you proper wire to patch up the breaks with?" I asked increduously.

"Yeah, I got a whole roll of it off 'em once."

"Well, what did you do with it?"

"Used some of it," said Scratcher, "And I sold some of it to me mates, I'm saving the rest. It's damn good wire, that. Copper, Comes in handy for binding up split axe-handles and oars and things."

"But where on earth do you get all this stuff?"

"Lying around," said Scratcher. "You'd be surprised what you can make do with."

"I *am* surprised," I said truthfully. "I've never seen anything like this in my bloody life."

"Mind you," warned Scratcher, "you can't go using just *any* old thing in a telephone line."

"No?"

"No fear," said Scratcher. "It's got to be *metal*."

"Has anyone else seen this?" I asked.

"No, I'm the only one who ever comes up here. As long as I keep their phone working okay nobody's got anything to worry about."

"I was beginning to see how old Scratcher worked. Although he was a dreadful scrounger he never had much of the fruits of his scavenging around his place because whatever he couldn't eat

151

he was hanging in the Tangaroa-Boulder Creek telephone line. If the people of Boulder Creek knew by what means their only link with the outside world was being maintained . . .

I later discovered another thing Scratcher used his roll of copper wire for. Sewing. Most of his buttons were tied on with it. And the sun glinting on the seams of his trousers or coat revealed that they, too were stitched up with telephone wire. He was the Roughest Bastard I've come across, old Scratcher, and I've come across some Rough Bastards in my time.

31
Literate Bastard

QUENTIN PARSONAGE WAS A tall, old, stooped bloke who used a shaving brush, and wore spectacles and sandals and an old grey suit when he went along to the Tangaroa pub or store. He lived with a green and yellow budgie called Mr Bo Jangles in a very tidy little place just inside the bush half a mile past the Tangaroa bridge. His place had been a shack when he moved into it, but he'd made it so neat and tidy that it was now a cottage. He was as fastidious as Scratcher Farrell wasn't, with everything scrubbed clean and put away in its proper place.

Quentin was a Real Literate Bastard (*Bastardus bookwormus*), who was always on the lookout for something to read. He had the biggest collection of old newspapers and magazines neatly stacked in his kitchen that anyone has ever seen, and Rex Logan, the local publican, reckoned that when Quentin first came to Tangaroa it only took him three weeks to read every printed word in the whole district. And to watch him actually read was rather interesting . . .

Bastardus bookwormus

it

looked

as

though

155

he

was

skimming

through

the

pages

as

quickly

as

this,

but

in fact he was reading every word as carefully as you're reading these ones. It's just that he was a terrifically fast reader. Sometimes he wouldn't even borrow a book, he'd read it right where it was, even if it took him two or three visits.

He inspected everything he handled to see what was written on it, and people didn't always understand why he examined their money so closely for something he'd bought. When he first came into a place he'd go round reading everything, like a dog sniffing. He read instructions, brand names and labels. He read the proof-marks on shotguns, and the *Made in Japan* stamped into the frames of fishing reels. He'd read your calendar, your cardboard boxes, the radio dial and the name on the fridge door. It only took him two trips between his place and the pub to polish off the whole dashboard, the warrant of fitness, the registration sticker, the lining of a hat, and the service manual I kept in the glovebox of the ute, but a war comic someone had left in my hut staggered him a bit. He fluttered through the pages and then dropped it into the fire as though to save anyone else from being exposed to it, which goes to show he was a man of taste. He liked to read everything but he didn't necessarily like everything he read.

He lived mainly on his pension, his garden and quite a few trout taken by various means from the river. And he drank mainly on anyone who would pay for his booze.

Sometimes when Quentin had a few rums under his belt he would entertain everyone with magician's tricks that mostly never quite came off. The first one I saw him make a botch of was the one where Quentin slipped a match up the hem of his handkerchief on the quiet and then showed everyone how he folded a match up in the handkerchief and broke it up inside it and then tipped it out again in one piece. You're supposed to break the match you've got up the hem of the handkerchief, but Quentin got the wrong one, three times in a row, and when he finally got it right no one was watching any more.

Then he tried the one about which cup the five cent piece was under, but he got confused and as often as not somebody else guessed it right. He dropped twenty cent pieces that were supposed to have disappeared, and forgot how to do tricks with matches arranged on the bar. He wasn't very good with tricks using bits of string either and he was useless at riddles and jokes because after an impressive and long-winded build-up he always forgot exactly how the punch-line went.

In short, Quentin was not only a Literate Bastard, but something of a Clumsy Bastard (*Bastardus ballsupus*) as well, as so many Literate or Intellectual Bastards — remember *Bastardus profoundus*? — are.

Quentin was worst of all with card tricks. Whenever a series of his tricks had let him down again, he'd call for the pack of cards Rex kept under the bar and get everyone ready to be shown a *real* trick. He'd finish off his rum and shuffle and snap the curled old pack and then lay out twenty-one cards on the bar like a Mississippi gambler in a movie and invite you to pick out any card you liked but not let on what it was. When you'd done that, he'd whisk them off the bar again, have another quick rum, shuffle the cards, and then slap them out again and ask you which row it was in now. He'd keep this up until you were beginning to lose interest, and then he'd suddenly flip a card out in front of you and say, "How's that?"

"No," you'd have to say.

Quentin would flip out another card as though the first one was just to get you guessing. "That it?" he'd say shrewdly.

"Nope."

"This one then . . ."

"Nope."

"Darn. I must have done something wrong. Hold on, I'll run through it again."

But he never got it right. The more he tried, the worse he got at it. It wasn't that he didn't *know* the tricks properly, it was because he had to have a fair few rums on board before he got up the courage to do them, and by that time he was starting to get a bit muddled.

He was good for business at the pub, though. Poeple who dropped in for a quick drink would sometimes stay for hours if Quentin was doing his tricks, fascinated by the gamble of whether he was going to get one of them right.

Everyone liked old Quentin and most of his carpentry and plumbing and fencing was done by blokes who'd dropped in to

161

see him and seen what a dreadful botch he was making of it. He was a hell of a good gardener though, grow anything. And he always had a cabbage or a couple of outsized lettuces to wrap up for you as you were leaving.

Quentin was the only one drinking in the pub when I turned up there one morning and Quentin had got straight on to the rum and was away to a great start. He'd brought a couple of enormous cabbages along for Rex Logan and had only just remembered to give them to him when I arrived.

"By strike," said Rex gratefully, pouring a double rum into Quentin's glass. "There's no doubt about you. You must put in more time in that garden of yours than a married man spends at home with the wife!"

"Naturally," said Quentin. "There's a lot more for a man in a garden than in a marriage."

"Get away with you," scoffed Rex. "You're a confirmed old batchelor, you are!"

"Oh, I've been married," said Quentin, replacing his empty glass on the bar.

"Fair go?" said Rex. "I never knew you'd been married."

"Oh yes," said Quentin.

"It's not worth mentioning," said Quentin, "I'd rather talk about gardening. It's more productive."

"Did you have any kids?" I asked, putting the money on the bar for another beer and motioning Rex to fill Quentin's glass as well.

"No, unfortunately," said Quentin.

"What happened?" asked Rex, giving them their drinks and leaning attentively on the bar.

"Oh, it was the usual exhausting treadmill," said Quentin. "Impossible to maintain. My wife was a very beautiful woman actually. A music teacher — well-educated."

Quentin paused for another drink.

"Before we were married," he went on, "she used to say I set her on fire. But after I married her all I found was a scattered heap of soggy embers that wouldn't ignite, no matter what I tried. But I'm not complaining. I was no better myself in a number of other ways."

"How do you mean?"

"Well, in my splendid self-sacrificing superiority, I'd gone and made an honest woman out of her. How grateful she would have to be! I'd married her, hadn't I? All I had to do now was sit back and spend the rest of my days receiving her spontaneous gratitude. But she let me down. Betrayed me. It wasn't like I'd expected it to be, whatever that was. Be so good as to give me another rum, please Rex." He interrupted himself. "A double, thanks."

"Yes, go on," prompted Rex, putting the drink on the bar and sliding the cloves bottle beside it without taking any money.

"Well," said Quentin, and he paused to polish off the rum, "I wasn't going to be treated like that. This woman I'd married not only didn't understand what I needed, but she wasn't giving it to me without my having to ask for it. I was forced to seek these unnameable things at the bosoms of the wife of a fellow lecturer at the university."

"Were you a lecturer at a university?" asked Rex incredulously.

"Senior lecturer in English at Canterbury," said Quentin.

"Well I'll be blowed," said Rex, "How long were you there?"

"Nine years," said Quentin, moving his empty glass on the bar so it'd be noticed. "After my divorce I left the university and took on private tutoring."

"What happened?" I asked. "Did you get caught with the lecturer's wife?"

"No, it wasn't like that," said Quentin. "It wasn't a matter of my wife finding out about it. She knew. All over the country there are men in all walks of life being unfaithful to their wives all the time. And all the women know it. But they can't do much about it because they don't feel what they're traditionally supposed to feel when their husbands take lovers. It's caused them to become better at concealing their husband's infidelities from themselves than the husbands are. There's not a woman alive who could stop loving a man she genuinely loves because of him having an affair with another woman, and yet for years she's been expected to divorce him for it. Of course I didn't realise all this when it was happening to me. I was doing what I was to make her sorry for what she was driving me to do so she'd change her

163

ways. And the more I did it, the more impossible it became for her to give me what I thought I needed so badly."

"What was that?" I asked.

"I'm not sure now, so I can't have had much idea at the time," said Quentin. "And it's as true of a marriage as of anything else that a thing that starts off on an illogical basis can never reach a logical conclusion. We tried to disregard this self-evident truth for three years and then we parted, complete strangers to one another. She went to live in Dunedin and from then on we only ever communicated through lawyers. The last time I saw her was in a courtroom getting her divorce and we were as close then as we'd ever been. — Excuse me, gentlemen. Nature calls." And he polished off his eleventh double rum for the day and left the bar.

"Good old Quentin," said Rex. "You know, he's been around here for over four years now and we never knew he'd ever been married, or a lecturer at a university.

"*Senior* lecturer," I said. "In English!"

"We knew he was well-educated," said Rex, "but this is the first time I've ever heard him talk about himself. What a bloke!"

Just then Quentin returned, a little unsteady on his feet, and said "Feel like a game of darts? I'll play you Aussie rules — lowest score pays for the drinks."

"Okay," I said. "You're on!"

But Quentin turned out to be such a rotten darts-player that I couldn't even contrive to lose a game to him. I was no great shakes at the game myself, but it was all Quentin could do to get one on the board. It didn't prevent us from having a very enjoyable session, though, and we arrived at Quentin's shack, both drunk and broke, in the middle of the afternoon for lunch.

Yes, he was a Real Literate Bastard was Quentin. I've always remembered what he had to say about women and marriage, and I really enjoyed the vegetables he cooked up for lunch.

Slow Bastard

EVERYONE RECKONED THAT WEAVER at the store had taken a shine to me, but the only indication I had of this was that Weaver was appearing a little sooner than usual when I went along there for supplies or petrol. Weaver was medium height and build, about middle-aged, with medium colouring and looks. He wore medium kind of clothes.

Somebody told me that Weaver used to be a dairy farmer, but he lost half his herd of cows in a poker-game with a couple of his neighbours, and couldn't afford to go on milking the rest. So he sold out and came to manage the Tangaroa store for six weeks while the owner found a permanent manager. After he'd been there a couple of years, he bought the place.

That was nineteen years ago. He hated Tangaroa and was always complaining about the "Godforsaken hole", but it was obvious that it was going to take him a while yet to move, for Weaver was a Real Slow Bastard (*Bastardus fullstopus*). I don't mean that he was retarded or anything like that; he just took his time to get moving. He owned half the property in Tangaroa by this time, and it didn't pay anyone to try and get him moving any faster than he felt like, which was never very fast. He had the only petrol for sixty miles, and people had been known to find themselves pleading with him to let them have a few gallons at any price because they'd been incautious enough to get uppity or impatient with him.

I had heard all about this, but I found it out for myself the day Weaver ordered me to come over to the house and have a bottle of beer with him. We were on our seventh or eighth bottle, sitting at Weaver's kitchen table, when a big American car pulled up at Weaver's petrol pump and a bloke in a grey suit and moustache got out and went into the store. After a while he came out again and spoke to his blue wife sitting in the car.

"Looks like he wants gas," I said.

Bastardus fullstopus

Weaver grunted and opened another bottle, filled his glass and slid the bottle across the table to me. Then Weaver's customer did a very tactless thing.

He blew the horn of his car.

Three times.

Weaver was drinking at the time and he paused with his glass held at his bottom lip while the horn was blowing and then he went on with his drink. We idly watched as the bloke looked at his watch and paced around in front of the store for a while and then came over the house and knocked on the door as though he had a search warrant. Weaver got up and went and opened the door.

"Do you sell petrol here?" demanded the bloke in a voice that was obviously used to running the show.

"Yeah," said Weaver, totally unimpressed or intimidated.

"Well I'll have four gallons, thank you," said the bloke.

Weaver grunted and shoved his feet into his boots on the porch and his customer led the way across to the petrol pump as though it was a race to get there first. But before he'd gone half-way Weaver was slapping his pockets. Then he stopped altogether.

"Hang on," he said, "I'll have to get me keys."

He took his boots off and came back into the house, finished his beer, put his boots on again and went back out to the pump. I went too.

Weaver unlocked the bowser and shoved the nozzle into the bloke's tank. But there wasn't enough juice in his batteries to run the electric motor in the petrol pump, so he hung the nozzle up again.

"I'll have to start the generator," he said patiently.

"Look here," said the bloke who wanted gas. "How long is this going to take? I'm in a hurry!"

"Dunno," said Weaver. "We'll have to see what kind of a mood the diesel's in." And we left his client mumbling something about ". . . old fool . . ." to his tight-lipped wife, and went round the back to start the generating plant.

Now it wasn't very often that Weaver had to start his generator in the daytime, so after we'd topped up the fuel tank and got her running, he did one or two minor adjustments he'd been

167

meaning to get on to, and by the time we got back round the front, his customer was standing by his car with his petrol cap in one hand and his wallet in the other.

Weaver's pump was one of the old ones, slow as hell. It clicked and dinged steadily over, tenth by tenth, until the four gallons were finally in the tank. By the time he'd hung up the nozzle the bloke was waving a five-dollar note in his face, but Weaver didn't see it until he'd got back from shutting off his generator.

"Two dollars, four cents," he said, reaching for the bloke's money.

"Just a minute," said the bloke, pulling his money away from Weaver's grasp. "That's fifty-one cents a gallon!"

"Yeah," said Weaver.

"But it's only forty-nine cents a gallon in Christchurch."

Weaver didn't bother explaining to him that the petrol had to be freighted to Tangaroa in forty-four gallon drums and siphoned into the reservoir under the pump at a cost in cartage and labour that more than covered the extra two cents a gallon he charged for it. He disappeared around the back and returned with a four-gallon tin and a piece of hose. He shoved the hose into the bloke's tank and started siphoning his gas out again.

"Hey," said the bloke when he saw what Weaver was doing. "What are you doing?"

"Not goin' t' force the stuff on y'," said Weaver. "If y' don't want it, I'll have it back again."

The bloke turned to me. "Is there anywhere else around here where I can buy petrol?" he asked.

"Nope," I said, shaking my head.

"But I haven't got enough to get me back to town," said the bloke.

"Weaver here sells it," I pointed out.

The bloke was beaten and he knew it.

"Look here," he said to Weaver in a very different tone of voice from the one he'd been using. "I didn't mean to imply that you were overcharging for your petrol. I realise that you have your expenses in a place like this . . ."

"You want it or don't you?" asked Weaver indifferently.

"I want it. I want it," said the bloke holding out his five dollars.

168

Weaver pulled his hose out of the bloke's tank, ran a dribble of petrol from it into his tin and took the money into the store. His far-from-satisfied customer took his change without counting it and drove back in the direction of town. I picked up Weaver's tin. Judging by its weight, it was half full.

"Did you charge him for the full four gallons, Weaver?"

"Yeah."

"But he only ended up with about two gallons."

Weaver grunted something or other and led the way back to his kitchen to fetch a bottle of beer. That sort of thing was nothing unusual to him.

"Everyone gets their money's worth around here," he said.

Weaver was a Slow Bastard, all right. I felt we could get on very well together.

Dale e Silmon

33
Useless Bastard

ANOTHER OF THE NOTEWORTHY citizens of Tangaroa was Ted Packer, a quaint old guy who leased the Muddy River flats for ninety-nine years. Ted was not so much one of the your Dozey Bastards (*Bastardus drippus*) or even a Lazy Bastard (*Bastardus loaferus*) like you or me. No, he was a Useless Bastard (*Bastardus nohopeus*), who ran about 200 tatty sheep and sixty-odd head of beef cattle, mostly on the road. His stock was always getting hit by cars or shot by spotlighters and his dogs were always hungry.

It was generally accepted that Ted was more concerned about his dogs than anything else he had, including his industrious little grey wife, who managed their property while Ted's seven or eight dogs only just managed to keep themselves from starving.

Ted always wore oilskins. Oilskin coat, oilskin sou'wester hat and oilskin leggings. And to see this lean weatherbeaten figure riding up the road on his tired, muddy, brown horse, attended by a retinue of hip-bony, ribby cattle-dogs, it was hard to imagine he wasn't arriving back from mustering all the chamois off the Southern Alps single-handed.

But he was probably just out for a ride and his wife had probably had to catch his horse for him and give him a leg up into the saddle because of his sciatica.

Actually Ted only ever rode along the road because his dogs were pretty good at getting themselves a feed of possum. And it was true that for three or four miles either side of his place there were usually frequent scatters of possum fur, where his dogs had dragged them out of the fern at the side of the road and cleaned up everything except some of the fur. You'd often come across him riding along with a few of his dogs coughing on fur and others still chewing on difficult parts of possum.

Every few days Ted would ride out and chase all his stock from one direction back towards home, but they always ran straight

Bastardus nohopeus

past his gate and in spite of all his dogs he didn't bother heading them off. He just chased them back the other way next time.

A Ministry of Works engineer complained in the pub one day that most of Ted Packer's stock had never set foot on his own property since they were calves or lambs. Once a year Ted trucked some of his stock away to a sale somewhere or other. At shearing time, dipping time, crutching time and lambing time — he didn't seem to bother.

Rex Logan swore that Ted hadn't been up his own river flats for so long that he didn't know his wife was breeding a big mob of mongrel horses up there. The horses and the deer were eating every blade of grass up Muddy River as fast as it would grow, so his stock only had the road to get a feed on anyway.

Rex reckoned that Ted was so much like one of his own dogs he couldn't even lie down without turning around a couple of times.

Ted didn't create a very good impression on passing traffic, either. They usually had to slow down to get past his dogs, who treated the road as their own personal domain, and people would often stop to ask this very colourful drover directions or questions about the district.

But Ted always told them about his sciatica instead, and then followed it up with how he was going to shoot the Governor-General when he got the chance because of something the Governor-General had said on the radio at Christmas time, 1956. And when they politely pointed out that we had a different Governor-General now, he'd say, "Arrgh, they're all the bloody same, them Governor-Generals. Just you let the bastard put one foot on my place, that's all! I'll drop him in his bloody tracks. I'll put one fair through his bloody guts for him! I'll . . ."

At about this point the travellers, who usually included a woman or two would politely thank him for his trouble and drive off wondering what the hell they'd struck.

No one knew what it was that the Governor-General had said on the radio at Christmas time in 1956 that had upset Ted so much, but since Ted's run-down property was so remote from anything that might be included in His Excellency's itinerary, he was unlikely to ever be in any danger from his arch-enemy, Ted Packer.

172

34

Indispensable Bastard

IF THE NEAREST THING in Tangaroa to a service station was Weaver's store, the nearest thing to a mechanic they had was Joe Bimler.

They've been saying no one's indispensable for so long now that we don't think about it any more, but I had occasion to reconsider that old saying the day I first saw Joe Bimler's workshop. If it was anything to do with cars or trucks, it was probably somewhere among the staggering conglomeration of spare parts that were hung, flung, or slung in Joe's big shed. But if you wanted to know *where* it was, then Joe Bimler was an absolutely Indispensable Bastard (*Bastardus necessarius*).

It was so difficult to accept that anyone could know exactly where everything was in that overwhelming mechanical morass, that you had to rediscover the fact that Joe could instantly tell you whether he had what you wanted or not, and then go and put his hand on it without even having to think where it was. In some incredibly complicated way the place, to him, was actually quite orderly. He'd shake a Commer fan-belt out of the tangle under the far end of the bench, or drag a Vauxhall gearbox out of the long grass behind the shed, as though he'd just put them there the day before yesterday. Joe himself was as deceptively untidy-looking as his workshop. A dark, loose-jointed, baggy, oily bloke, completely uncorrupted by any kind of formal training or education, he'd been married for a few years, but his wife had turned it in and gone back to live with her parents in Motueka.

He had a fleet of four old trucks — starting from number forty-five and only one of them was actually on the road at any one time, but he could only drive one of them at a time anyway, and he was probably the only man alive who could have driven them safely over those roads. With five yards of wet shingle on the back he could pull one of his trucks up from thirty to a dead stop using nothing but the gearbox and the soft going at the side

173

Bastardus necessarius

of the road. His brakes were notoriously in need of adjustment or repair. They reckoned he'd wear out three clutch pedals before his brake pedal was even shiny.

He hired out his trucks to the Ministry of Works on road work between Greymouth and Tangaroa, though his schedule was a bit unreliable because of his frequent stops for roadside repairs and him having to do most of his travelling at night. Something to do with Certificates of Fitness and Registration and other such formalites.

Joe had once been caught by the M.O.W. engineer who'd hired him, giving his truck a valve-grind on the job. They fired him, but then had to re-hire him because the nearest other truck would have had to travel more than eighty miles to get to and from the job.

Joe was an obliging bloke and he'd cheerfully fix your car for you, if it could be fixed, though unless it was a V8 he was inclined to diagnose the trouble, whatever it was, as being directly traceable to a chronic lack of power. Straight-sixes weren't quite so bad, but he treated anything with four cylinders with utter contempt. Scratcher came into the pub one day with his leathery old feelings hurt because Joe had just told him his Land Rover couldn't pull a hen off its roost.

But there wasn't a mechanic or engineer in the country who could touch Joe Bimler on V8 motors. Give him a V8 and he'd do things with it that would defy every specification the manufacturers darted to claim for it. If the makers' recommended maximum revs-per-minute were 3,500, Joe would get her doing 5,000 just to test her before he slapped her into one of his old trucks.

Or he'd take one that someone had worn out and thrown away, do her up a bit, and get another 50,000 miles out of it.

When Joe was winding up one of his V8s to check her out, the whole village stopped in its tracks. He'd stand there and open her up like a siren, until he produced a high-pitched shriek of a sound that was almost beyond the range of the human ear. And he'd hold it there until you'd swear something had to blow up any second.

Anyone standing round watching moved further back out of

175

the way. Business at the pub and the store, half a mile away, came to an uneasy standstill. Dogs set up a howling that travelled as far as Boulder Creek. Deer, 3,000 feet up in the Alps, stopped feeding, looked about them with a startled air, and then hurried off into thick cover on the far side of the ridge. The bird-life was stunned into silence for the rest of the day, completely upstaged. Small animals in their burrows and tree-holes and nests got such a fright that there wasn't a possum to be seen on the road for the next three nights. The sandflies stopped biting. The trout in the Tangaroa River moved into deeper water. If it was raining it stopped and if it wasn't raining it started. The trees in the forest produced wavery growth-rings, and dislodged rocks bounded in panic down the sides of the mountains.

Joe, the maestro of the whole ear-splitting performance, stood calmly beside his madly vibrating and leaping machine with the throttle in one hand and a screwdriver in the other, making one or two final adjustments to the mixture or the timing.

The silence when he finally let the whole district off the hook was uncanny. An hour or so after it stopped Joe would drive up the road in one of his trucks and stop outside the pub, give her one or two unnerving bursts of acceleration and come into the bar looking as pleased with himself as though he'd just inherited a whole Ford factory.

"Just slapped a new motor in old forty-seven," he'd announce superfluously. "She should be okay for a while now."

"I certainly hope so," said the publican. "The last time you put a motor in one of your trucks me chooks went off the lay for a fortnight."

It was Joe who gave me the most hair-raising ride in a motor vehicle I've ever had in my life. I was half a mile up the riverbed getting a load of firewood in my ute and on my way back I tore the sump off on an ordinary bunch of reeds that turned out to be growing around a petrified knot of red beech as hard as iron.

Luckily I stopped to see what the bang was and found all my sump-bolts stripped out of the block and the badly-dented sump lying just in front of a rear wheel. I walked all the way out to the road and along to the pub. After a quick beer I went along

176

to Joe's place and found him working on an old hydraulic hoist he'd picked up somewhere. I explained to Joe what had happened.

"Yair," said Joe. "I've done one or two of 'em before. We'll just have to straighten out your sump and tap out bigger holes in the block and slap her on with bigger bolts. They're usually quarter-inch, so five-sixteenth ought to do it. I've got some here."

"Do you think you could tow me off the riverbed?" I asked. "She's out on the shingle below flood level."

"Sure, we'll go and drag her in and do the job right here."

Joe threw a huge snigging-chain on to the back of his currently-functioning V8 truck and off we roared to get my ute. Bouncing out across the riverbed I had to hang onto the glovebox hole in the dashboard to keep myself from being flung into the door or the windscreen or Joe. We backed up to the ute and shackled Joe's big snigging-chain around my front axle and on to a rear spring-hanger of Joe's truck.

"I'll have to keep us moving once we get going across this shingle," said Joe. "If we break through the surface of this stuff we'll both be stuck here."

"Well, okay," I said, "but take it easy on my waggon, will you?"

"Okay," said Joe, opening his truck door. "You right?"

"Yep."

When people say they're going to take off in a motor vehicle they usually only mean that they're going to *move* off along the road, on the surface of the earth. Joe used the term literally.

He took off across the riverbed without even taking up the slack in the chain first. I was plucked from a standstill to full revs of Joe's truck in second gear so suddenly it almost broke my neck. And I never regained proper control of the ute during the whole of that terrible ride.

We careered over the riverbed at a speed that made it impossible for me to think. I slewed from side to side, frantically spinning the wheel one way and then the other to save myself from hitting into the logs and bigger rocks Joe was casually dodging around. We bounced on to the track and out to the main road up a foot-high bank that tore the steering-wheel out of my grasp,

177

and one of the spokes hit my thumb with the force of a backfiring crank-handle.

As soon as we were on the track Joe slammed his truck into third gear with a jerk that must have almost ripped the whole front suspension out of the ute. A little later I found myself seriously wishing it had done.

I just couldn't get control of my vehicle for more than a few seconds at a time. Whenever Joe steered around a pothole or corner, my wagon would start swerving violently from one side to the other. At one point, my off-side wheels rode up on an overgrown log beside the track and the ute rose up to the very point of rolling over, but Joe's big chain dragged me back on to my wheels with a spine-jolting bang that shot me into the scrub on the other side of the track.

Now, I'd travelled that track many times, and I thought I knew it well, but I was getting a vastly different view of it that day. My only indication that we'd reached the main road was when Joe started crashing his truck down through its gearbox. I felt some relief — surely the main road would be easier going!

But we bounced out on to the road, regardless of anything that might be coming and took off towards Tangaroa with the chain flailing around in front of my bonnet. Second — third — top gear, and Joe was flat to the boards. At one point I was sideways-on to Joe's truck and almost parallel with his tailboard. I could see Joe's face in the rear-vision mirror, but Joe wasn't looking back, and then I was snatched round out of a skid and started on another one in the other direction.

Whenever I could spare a hand I kept it on the horn or banged on the side of the ute with it, but Joe couldn't have heard anything over the unmuffled roar of his hurtling truck. It was too dangerous to even jump out. The only thing I had in favour of my survival was that I had brakes and Joe didn't but I was too frightened to touch them.

As far as I knew things couldn't have been much worse, but during a particularly violent swerve out on to the wrong side of the road, I was horrified to see Scratcher's old Land Rover approaching.

So this was to be the way I went out. I didn't even bother

178

getting ready to meet my Maker. There was nothing he could do anyway.

Ever since that day I've often wondered at the trivial kind of thing that can settle a man's fate. What, for instance, if Scratcher had set off from wherever he did a few seconds earlier or later?

But as it happened, I was just swinging out from behind Joe's truck when Scratcher went past. I caught a fractional glimpse of him meandering along with one hand still raised in a wave to Joe and the other absently picking his nose, as I was hurled past the outside corner of the Land Rover, missing it by a margin as minute as the fact that Scratcher's bomb needed a coat of paint.

The only other near-casualties of the journey were a couple of pub verandah-posts. I was too physically and emotionally exhausted to register a serious complaint when we finally pulled up at Joe's place. The ute was covered with mud and scratches. There was fern and scrub hanging off the bumpers and door-handles and windscreen wipers. Both parking lights and one headlight were broken. Its mudguard and grille had been flogged by Joe's chain until their original shapes were only distinguishable by comparison with another vehicle of the same make and model. My outside rear-vision mirror had been torn off, but apart from that, the ute had hung together remarkably well.

In such ways as this, the greatest film sequences of our times are lost to us.

I was in about the same condition as my ute. My thumb was sprained and swelling; one of my elbows was still hurting from a crack on the window-winder; some skin had been bruised off one of my knees on the bottom edge of the dashboard; I had a bruise on my forehead, and I'd bitten my tongue.

"Didn't you hear me blowing the horn?" I asked Joe.

"No," said Joe, "but it wouldn't have made any difference. You couldn't have got past me anyway."

"No," I agreed.

Joe had the sump straightened out and back on the ute and topped up with oil out of his own drum within an hour. He even managed to get the worst dents knocked out of the mudguard and grille, and Joe found a headlight unit to replace the one that had got broken. He refused to accept any payment for his time and trouble, so I thanked him as warmly as I could and drove slowly to the pub for a very quiet drink.

My driving was anxiously over-cautious for as long as my wheel-marks stayed all over the sides of the road to remind me. It was months before they were all washed away by the rains and I could begin to forget about it a little, and there were times when I concluded that Joe was definitely a Dispensable Bastard, (*Bastardus giveawayus*).

35
Stupid Bastard

EGGY NEWBIGAN WAS NOT so much a Stupid Bastard (*Bastardus clottus*) as a Dangerous Bastard (*Bastard suicidus*), but I suppose that we'd better give him the benefit of the doubt. Eggy was a good name for him for he looked a bit of an egg — let's face it, he *was* an egg, and a proper bloody egg at that. He'd been around Tangaroa for two or three years, doing odd work that nobody else wanted to do. They'd given him a job maintaining a stretch of road but he'd filled all the pot-holes with dirt out of the water-tables and they knew better than to let him near any machinery, so he'd had to be sacked.

Weaver gave him a trial week looking after the store, but within three days Eggy had got the cash register and the shelves in such a confusion that it took Weaver a month to get them right again. He figures that Eggy must have eaten eighteen dollars worth of chocolate and sweets and had to write them off, along with Eggy.

Rex Logan at the pub, against everyone's advice, let Eggy have a go at looking after the bar, but nobody wanted to drink with him there and he had to be put on general work around the place. He rearranged all Rex's stocks of bottles and stuff and Rex couldn't find anything when he wanted it. It took poor Rex three weeks to get exasperated enough to sack Eggy, and by that time he'd burnt holes and grooves in shelves, benches, floors, tables, mats, bedclothes, and books, by leaving his lighted cigarette-butts everywhere. He'd broken glass all over the place, including a big window; he'd set fire to the pub twice, trying to light the fire in the bar with newspaper; he'd tied the pub goat within reach of Mrs Logan's washing; he'd dropped the telephone and broken that; he'd driven Rex's car into the bench at the end of the car-shed and even Joe Bimler couldn't fix it without sending up to town for parts; he'd left the beer tap dribbling one night on a nearly-full eighteen-gallon keg and flooded half the building with beer. And he'd made the pub leak in several places by walking

Bastardus clottus

all over the corrugated-iron looking for one of Rex's slippers he'd accidentally thrown on to the roof . . . All in all he'd been more trouble that he was worth, as usual.

He'd nearly shot Ted Packer with a rifle, so he wasn't very popular in that quarter. And he'd spilt one of Joe Bimler's drums of diesel into the river last whitebait season, which didn't raise his shares with anyone else.

Quentin Parsonage was the last Tangarorian to have lost faith in Eggy Newbigan. He stuck up for him when everyone else was well and truly convinced that Eggy was absolutely hopeless. He responded to Eggy's critics by saying that, after all, there's a little bit of good and a little bit of bad in all of us. And then Eggy rode a horse through Quentin's vegetable garden and Quentin came into the pub with his sandals flapping angrily and his spectacles fairly blazing with indignation. Eggy was leaning patiently on the bar waiting for Rex Logan to change his mind and give him a beer on credit.

"Egbert," said Quentin. "Did you ride your horse through my garden yesterday?"

"Yeah," said Eggy. "I did have a bit of a look around. You weren't there."

"Is that any reason to ride a horse all over my plants?"

"I don't know," said Eggy. "I didn't take much notice."

"Well don't come to my place ever again," said Quentin. "I don't want you there. You are a *wretched* fellow!" he repeated.

And Eggy had lost his only ally in Tangaroa, or probably anywhere else for that matter. And yet he still thought he was popular with everyone.

I should have known better, but when Eggy offered to let me go fifty-fifty on a scrap metal contract he'd got with a North Island company, I agreed to have a look at it. Eggy was lifting four miles of narrow-gauge tramline that ran back into the bush from the old mill, which was two miles north of Tangaroa and half a mile down a side road. Eggy had already sent the first load of tramlines away and had a cheque for seventy dollars to prove it.

It should have been a good lurk. The old jigger-wheels were still there and all it needed was to make up a jigger to wheel the tramlines on as they were lifted. The only snag was that Eggy had taken his first load from the rails nearest the road, instead of bringing them from the far end. The closest rails left were a quarter of a mile back in the swampy bush. He'd loused that job up as well.

Everyone seeemed to think that I should thank my lucky stars that Eggy had mucked up the job before I had put any money or work into it, but I couldn't help pointing out to Eggy what he'd done wrong and that the only way to put it right was to bring rails forward and rebuild the stretch he'd lifted, so he could get them all in to the mill. And a week later Eggy walked all the way down to my place to tell me he'd done as I'd suggested; he'd re-laid the quarter-mile of tramlines he'd taken out first.

The only thing wrong was that he'd re-laid them from the *second* quarter-mile of the line.

It's never easy to be tolerant of such idiocy, but I managed to explain to Eggy that he should have taken the rails from the *last*, the farthest away, end of the line first. I eventually seemed to have got the message across and left Eggy preparing to make himself a jigger and take it right to the end of the line and bring in the rails to bridge the second gap he'd made.

Ten days or so later I heard that Eggy had at last got his tramline-salvage job organised workably, but by this time the truck had been back three times to pick up the second load. They were so sick of the waste of their time and money that they'd dropped the project altogether.

But Eggy went on bringing in the tramlines until he had tons of them lying in great tangled heap on the old mill-skids. All he ever sold them was one rail, to Scratcher for two dollars. (It's probably now part of the Tangaroa-Boulder Creek telephone line.)

Scratcher and I were going spotlighting and as we were getting ready to leave the pub Eggy started hanging about wanting to come, so I eventually said he could come and hold the light for us.

"No!" said Weaver, who'd been listening to our preparations.

But Eggy was finally allowed to come providing he didn't touch any rifles and did what he was told. Weaver still wasn't happy about it. Half an hour after we'd got going Scratcher banged on the roof and I stopped and got out. Scratcher had a set of deer's eyes holding well in the powerful light, high up on a slip in the bush above the road. I leaned on the ute, hissed at Eggy to keep quiet and still, and pulled off a fine shot. The deer dropped in its tracks.

Scratcher and I took the torch and left Eggy to keep the spotlight on the spot where the deer had gone down. But Eggy started waving the light around all over the place so we just carried on with our torch. We found the deer, a young stag, lying in a muddy waterhole at the bottom of the slip. We pulled it out and gutted it and rolled and dragged it down to the road. There was no spotlight at all by this time. Eggy had shorted it somehow and blown the bulb.

There was nothing to do but go back to the pub, so we told Eggy to stay on the back and off we went. But we'd only just got going when there was an explosion and a shout, so I jammed on the brakes and jumped out. Eggy had been getting the rifle ready, in case we saw a deer on the road, and he'd put a .303 bullet through the bonnet of the ute and out through the radiator. We took the rifle off him and sat him in the front where we could keep an eye on him, and made it back to the pub without overheating the ute too much.

Joe Bimler was at home and apparently only too pleased to have something to fix, so we left him hunched over my radiator with a soldering-iron and Scratcher drove Eggy and me home in his Land Rover.

Next morning I arrived at Joe's place to pick up the ute and found that Eggy had been there for about an hour already, to lend a hand. He'd been hosing down the muddy deer on the back of the ute, and he'd left the hose running. Everything was drenched and the deer was unsellable. It had gone soggy.

And Eggy had left the hose running when Joe had had to leave for work and taken him home rather than leave him there. But Eggy had walked back and was there to lend a hand when I tried to back my ute out. It slid sideways in the mud and ended up hard against Joe's gatepost. And while I was away getting Scratcher and his Land Rover, Eggy jacked up some wire-strainers and fencing wire he found in Joe's shed and pulled the door handle off the ute trying to drag it away from the post for me.

185

Scratcher and I arrived back just in time. Eggy had his wire tied on to the steering wheel and already had it sprung to its limits through the window.

We chased the Stupid Bastard away up the road with a stick, throwing rocks and abuse after him, and got the ute out without any further damage.

After that I followed everyone else's example and wouldn't let Eggy hang around anywhere near me, and only had the average number of calamities to cope with.

Bitch list

Lieth